12-WEEK
Partner
RECOVERY
GUIDE

Journey To Healing from Sexual Betrayal

Beth Denison, CLC, PRC, CPC-C

12-Week Partner Recovery Guide

Beth Denison

Published by Austin Brothers Publishing,
Fort Worth, Texas
www.abpbooks.com

ISBN 978-1-7333130-6-3
Library of Congress Control Number 2020909524
Copyright © 2020 by Beth Denison

Unless otherwise indicated, Scripture quotations are from the Holy Bible, New International Version, copyright 1973, 1978, 1984 by Biblica, Inc."

Printed in the United States of America
2020 -- First Edition

This book is dedicated to . . .

My God, who filled me with hope when I had none, gave me the strength to persevere, and redeemed for his glory what the enemy meant for my destruction. I am nothing without him.

My husband and best friend of 37 years, Mark, who is my greatest encourager and without whom I would have never completed this project.

My amazing son, David, whose deep exploration of Scripture, Christ-like forgiveness, and positive spirit inspire me to be a better person.

Table of Contents

INTRODUCTION

Betrayal – with its discovery comes an unbelievable pain that reaches to the core of our being, bringing suffering that makes us feel like our hearts are shattering into a million pieces. There is the realization that life as we've known it is over. If you are reading this workbook, you have likely experienced this kind of devastation. For that, I'm profoundly sorry.

You are not alone. Millions of individuals have experienced the pain caused by the infidelity of a spouse or partner. This may include sexual fantasy, pornography, masturbation, cybersex, strip clubs, massage parlors, physical or emotional affairs, prostitutes, or any number of other sexual activities.

Regardless of the method of your loved one's sexual acting out, you are left standing in the wreckage with a heart full of emotions and a mind filled with questions. This is worsened by the fact that like the majority of betrayed partners, you may be experiencing post-traumatic stress symptoms similar to that of a rape victim or a soldier returning from combat.

You may be struggling to imagine how you can possibly survive this trauma. You can do more than just survive. You can laugh, dream, and trust again. You cannot predict or control the outcome for your partner. He or she may not choose recovery. The end of *your* story is yet to be written. You can choose to walk a path of healing.

Over the next twelve weeks, I will provide you with tools essential for your recovery. I so wish I could tell you that by the end of our work together you will be healed from the pain of betrayal. Unfortunately, that is probably unrealistic. But I can tell you that if you do this work, incorporate into your daily life the things you learn from it, and continue to make recovery work a priority, you will be on a solid path toward healing.

We know that the majority of those struggling with sexually compulsive or addictive behaviors are men. Therefore, for purposes of this workbook, I will be addressing the wife as the wounded spouse. But the numbers are quickly changing as more and more women are viewing pornography and are involved in the same sexual acting out activities as men. This has resulted in a rapidly growing number of men left to deal with the effects of betrayal.

The actions of your partner may have thrown you into a pit of despair, but it's not God's intent for you to live there. In this dark place, whether you are a wife or a husband who has been devastated by infidelity, trust the Light of the world to lead you out of the pit and into a brighter future.

Let's get started.

WEEK ONE
Recovery

"I'm not telling you it is going to be easy.
I'm telling you it's going to be worth it."

- Anonymous

Day One
Trauma

"If my spouse is the one with the problem, why do I need to be in recovery?" This is a common question from someone married to a sex addict. Unfortunately, much of the material that has previously been written for the partner of an addict is done from a viewpoint that she is codependent and thus bears some responsibility for her husband's cycle of addiction. This inflicts further pain and can leave the wife convinced she is either complicit and in need of recovery work or that she is not codependent and therefore her spouse is the only one who needs to be in recovery.

So, if you don't consider yourself to be codependent, why should you be in recovery?

YOU'VE EXPERIENCED TRAUMA.

Trauma – a wound, either physical or psychological, caused by a singular incident or recurring events that caused the victim to feel fear, helplessness and loss of control, eventually impacting the individual's body, mind, and emotions such that the ability to cope was threatened.

Trauma Symptoms

Hypervigilance	Shock
Worry	Difficulty sleeping
Difficulty concentrating	Anxiety
Fear	Confusion
Difficulty remembering	Panic attacks
Intrusive thoughts	Denial
Emotional numbness	Feelings of shame
Irritability	Racing heart
Upset stomach	Anger
Sadness	Fatigue
Depression	Overeating
Withdrawal	No appetite

Everybody responds in his or her own way. This is not an exhaustive list, but these are some of the more common symptoms. On Day Two, we will consider where to go from here.

Day One Assignments

The Bible tells the story in I Kings of a prophet named Elijah who experienced trauma. Jezebel, the wife of evil king Ahab, vowed to have Elijah killed because he orchestrated a showdown between Jehovah God and the false god of Baal, whom she served, in which God displayed his power over Baal, leading Elijah to have the false prophets killed.

"Elijah was afraid and ran for his life. When he came to Beersheba in Judah, he left his servant there, while he himself went a day's journey into the wilderness. He came to a broom bush, sat down under it and prayed that he might die. 'I have had enough, Lord,' he said. 'Take my life; I am no better than my ancestors.' Then he lay down under the bush and fell asleep. All at once an angel touched him and said, 'Get up and eat.' He looked around, and there by his head was some bread baked over hot coals, and a jar of water. He ate and drank and then lay down again" (I Kings 19:3-6).

In this short passage, I see at least ten symptoms of trauma exhibited by Elijah: fear and panic as he ran for his life; withdrawal as he leaves his servant and goes off alone; depression and resignation as he prays to die; shame as he compares himself to his unfaithful ancestors; extreme fatigue as he does nothing but sleep; lack of appetite as he apparently had not eaten anything; and difficulty remembering, as it doesn't occur to him that if God gave him victory over 450 false prophets, surely he could protect him from one woman.

You're experiencing the trauma caused by betrayal, and likely, you can identify with Elijah. Perhaps you even think death is the only escape from the pain. God sees your distress, hears your cries and feels your pain. He will minister to you as he did to Elijah, if you'll let him.

Questions

1. At any point, have you questioned why you should participate in recovery, reasoning your husband is the only one with issues? Yes ☐ No ☐

2. If so, have you resolved that question? How? _____

    _____

    _____

    _____

3. Which trauma symptoms listed on Day One are you experienc-
    ing? _____

    _____

    _____

Next Step: Pray and ask God to help you fully embrace recovery and to strengthen you for the long road ahead.

Day Two
The Pit of Betrayal

"I waited patiently for the Lord; he turned to me and heard my cry. He lifted me out of the slimy pit, out of the mud and mire; he set my feet on a rock and gave me a firm place to stand" (Psalm 40:1-2).

The psalmist found himself in a pit, unable to get out on his own. In his pain and distress, he cried out to God. Perhaps you can relate to the writer's desperation. The discovery of sexual betrayal has you feeling like you're alone in a dark hole, seemingly with no way out. Maybe you, too, have cried out to God but have yet to be rescued. What can we learn from the psalmist's experience that might help in this painful time?

Lessons From the Pit

1. You did nothing to cause this.

Nothing you did or didn't do justifies the addict's destructive choices.

2. God has not abandoned you.

When you discover your spouse has betrayed you, it is easy to feel alone and question God's place in this situation. On multiple occasions in the Bible, God said, *"I will never leave you nor forsake you."* God did not cause your spouse to betray you nor did he prevent it, because he has created each of us with the freedom to make our own choices. To prevent your situation, God would have had to violate that principle. Your spouse has not only betrayed you, he has betrayed the perfect, holy God.

3. You can't be unscathed after a fall into the pit.

The victim in the Psalm was disoriented by the fall, knocked off his feet and covered in mud. You have been adversely affected also.

4. You can't climb out on your own.

You're stuck in the mud. Surrendering to God is your only way out.

5. Becoming a victim is not a choice but remaining one is.

Just as God did not force your spouse to make healthy choices, he will not force you to, either. You are free to wallow in the mud of self-pity, refusing to accept God's way out.

6. God sees your situation and hears your cries.

"Then why doesn't he rescue me now and take the pain away?" What God allows, he will redeem and use for your good and his glory. But first, there is a work he must do in and around you.

7. God will lift you out of the pit but it won't happen quickly.

Notice the writer of Psalm 40 had to wait. You will, too. There is healing that must take place before you can once again stand.

8. The process of healing extends beyond the initial crisis.

The Lord rescued the victim out of the pit and placed him on a firm place to stand. But additional healing was necessary before he was able to walk again. It is tempting when things begin to stabilize after the initial crisis to think we no longer need to remain in recovery. Failure to continue the work will likely result in a failure to completely heal.

Day Two Assignments

1. Have you blamed yourself for your husband's addiction with the "If only I had _____" types of statements? List a couple of those that come to mind. _____

   _____

   _____

   _____

2. Have you blamed God for your husband's choices?
   Yes ☐ No ☐ Explain your answer. _____

   _____

   _____

   _____

3. Are you ready to surrender to God's way out of the pit?
   Yes ☐ No ☐ What, if any, reservations do you have? _____

   _____

   _____

   _____

Next Step: Pray a prayer of surrender, committing to following God's way out of the pit instead of whatever way you may think is best. Ask him for the patience to trust his timing through the process. Ask him to remove the lies of self-blame from your mind.

Day Three
Healing the Wounds

There is an old saying that time heals all wounds. Unfortunately, that is not true. The mere passing of time will not heal the wounds you've endured as a result of your spouse's sexual acting out.

Jay Marshall said, "The truth is that time does not heal anything. It merely passes. It is what we do during the passing of time that helps or hinders the healing process."

As we established on Day Two, you've been thrown in the pit of betrayal. While it may be technically possible to be thrown into a pit without experiencing considerable damage, it is highly unlikely. So, what is going to be different in your life one year from now?

Your spouse may or may not choose to fully embrace recovery and diligently stay the course for the next year. You have no control over that. But you can heal even if he doesn't. How will that happen? Will it happen if you just try to ignore the situation and stuff the painful emotions? A broken bone may eventually mend without medical care, but it will likely take longer, hurt more, be incomplete and result in future complications.

Real and lasting healing is possible. But I would be less than honest if I did not tell you that things often get worse before they get better, the work is difficult and painful, and the process is slow. No matter how dire your circumstances appear, there are no hopeless situations from God's standpoint. Jesus said, *"With man this is impossible, but with God all things are possible"* (Matthew 19:26).

What is required to experience healing? First, you have to choose to believe God's word over your own feelings. Many times you will feel hopeless and you will be tempted therefore to believe it is hopeless. Second, you have to put in the work. Taking the time to read recovery materials every day, doing the exercises, going to meetings, talking to the therapist or coach, and processing painful emotions, doesn't usually fit conveniently into our schedule. It requires sacrifice. Finally, you have to persevere. It gets old and can be frustrating when you don't see it making a difference. *"Let us not become weary in doing good, for at the proper time we will reap a harvest if we do not give up"* (Galatians 6:9).

Healing the wounds caused by sexual betrayal is difficult. But it is possible. It will require a lot of work. But it is worth it. Is there really a price too high for living a life of victory? Your only alternative is living your life as a victim. It is your choice.

Day Three Assignments

I am not a gardener. No one has ever accused me of having a green thumb. Frankly, what happens to plants in my care is best described as inhumane. It is not that I don't like plants or that I don't want a nice garden. But somehow my mere desire and minimal effort do not result in a beautiful garden.

Imagine my delight when we moved into our current house and there was a lovely Hibiscus plant in my front flower bed. I've done nothing to it and it continues to look decent. Concluding that this plant must do well under the sole care of God, I decided to buy a nice pot and plant a Hibiscus in it to place on our back patio. Guess what happened? Yep, God dropped the ball with this one.

The reality is that someone likely prepared the soil and diligently cared for the one I acquired when we bought our house and it has a healthy root system that has served it well to this point. The one I haphazardly threw in a pot, while hoping for the best, didn't have the same advantage.

There was a preacher who saved up enough money to buy some cheap land. On it stood a dilapidated farmhouse. For a year, the preacher refurbished the house on his days off. Once the work was complete, a neighbor came over and said, "Well, preacher, I have to hand it to you. It looks like you and the Lord have done a pretty good job with this place."

Wiping the sweat from his brow, the preacher said, "Yeah, I suppose we have. But you should have seen the place when the Lord had it all to himself."

God could choose to just heal your wounds instantly. But he likely won't. You will have to make the decision and then partner with him to consistently do the hard work. Only then will you reap the reward of a life healed and will others marvel at the result.

Questions

1. How does it make you feel to hear that healing from the wounds of sexual betrayal is hard work, requires sacrifice, and takes a considerable amount of time? _____

   _____

   _____

   _____

2. Have you experienced feelings of hopelessness?
   Yes □ No □ How do you combat those feelings? _____

   _____

   _____

   _____

Next Step: Decide to fully embrace your own recovery and then roll up your sleeves and partner with God to do the work required to make healing part of your reality.

Day Four
First Step, Get in Touch with Reality

"Let no one deceive you with empty words" (Ephesians 5:6).

It would be foolish to marry someone who is a habitual liar. It is natural to expect a spouse to be honest. However, issues arise when that spouse is an addict. In addition to destructive and hurtful acting out behaviors, addicts lie. And they lie a lot. In fact, lying usually becomes so second nature with an addict that he will lie about things that have no consequence.

The addict lives in two worlds and becomes adept at compartmentalizing them. There is the world you know that includes you as his wife, his family, his job, and his community. Separately, at least in the addict's mind, there exists a secret world where he lives out his sexual addiction, whatever form that may take. When his two worlds begin to collide, the addict lies to preserve the two.

This is usually the point when you, as the spouse, begin to doubt your reality. There are things that don't add up – explanations that don't make sense. When an addict is confronted with these inconsistencies, he usually responds out of what Dr. Doug Weiss labeled his **verbal reality**. In this verbal reality, if the addict says it, it is true and the more passionately he says it, the truer it is. This leaves the spouse with two choices: trust her husband or trust her intuition and logic. These incongruencies often leave the wife feeling crazy or confused.

What then are you as the wife to do? Instead of relying solely on his words, believe his behavior. It is the true indicator. If the addict says he wants the marriage to survive and is willing to pursue recovery, look for the behaviors that validate the words. Is he going to 12-step meetings, reading recovery materials, working with a sponsor, seeing a therapist, and being accountable to you and another person? **Behavioral reality** is the true measure of recovery.

Day Four Assignments

One of the most heartbreaking examples of lying in the Bible is the story about the apostle Peter denying Christ and lying about even knowing him. Jesus had warned Peter that he would deny him three times. When Jesus was arrested, Peter followed behind and sat outside in the courtyard near where Jesus was being held. While there, he was asked three times about having been with Jesus and each time he denied it. On the third time, Peter was vehement in his response. The Bible says, *"Then he began to call down curses, and he swore to them, 'I do not know the man!'"* (Matthew 26:74).

Friedrich Nietzsche said, "No man lies so boldly as the man who is indignant." This is often true of the addict. In his verbal reality, the more passionately he states something, the truer it is. Believe his behavior over his words. *"Produce fruit in keeping with repentance"* (Matthew 3:8). The Bible is clear that the mark of true change is not the words one says, but the works that follow.

This is not just true for the addict. It must be true for you as well. It is easy to say you want to heal from the betrayal trauma you're experiencing, but are you doing the things that are necessary for that to happen? Are you reading recovery materials, going to meetings, seeing a therapist, working with a sponsor, and doing assignments? Your behavior is the true indicator.

Questions

1. Have you had periods in which the disconnect between your husband's words and reality made you feel crazy? Yes ☐ No ☐

2. When confronting your husband about your suspicions, has he ever suggested you were the crazy one, and if so, how did that make you feel? Did it cause you to doubt yourself? _____
   _____
   _____
   _____

3. Do your words regarding your desire for recovery match your actions? If not, what changes do you need to make? _____

_____

_____

Next Step: Don't listen to your husband's words about his recovery. Watch his actions and take note of his attitude. Make sure your own behavior supports your words, as well.

Day Five
Self-Care

"The apostles gathered around Jesus and reported to him all they had done and taught. Then, because so many people were coming and going that they did not even have a chance to eat, he said to them, 'Come with me by yourselves to a quiet place and get some rest'" (Mark 6:30-31).

Most women, especially mothers, tend to do a good caring for everyone else. But when it comes to ourselves, we often neglect our own needs, believing to do otherwise is selfish and unimportant. If we are going to continue caring for our loved ones and managing our other responsibilities, plus work on our recovery, now especially, we need to nourish ourselves spiritually, physically, mentally, and emotionally. The damage caused by a husband's marital betrayal affects the wife on all levels. Self-care, especially during this time, is not just important; it can be critical. So what does that look like?

1. **Spiritual Connection** - There is nothing that can shatter a heart into a thousand pieces and cause you to want to withdraw from all the world quite like discovering the love of your life has been unfaithful. What you most need then is to turn to God.

    "The Lord is close to the brokenhearted and saves those who are crushed in spirit" (Psalm 34:18).

    No one else can comfort like God and no one else has the power to do the impossible. Talk to God. Tell him about your hurt and fears. Ask him to give you the strength to make it through this difficult time.

2. **Physical Well-Being** - All trauma takes a toll on our physical bodies. It is important to do those things that ensure our health.
    a. Get tested. This is one time when believing the addict's words could cost you your health and even your life. Make an

appointment with your doctor as soon as possible to be tested for STDs.

b.   Get plenty of sleep. Stress is exhausting and you won't be able to think clearly and make good choices if you are sleep deprived. If you are consistently unable to sleep, talk to your doctor about getting a sleep aid.

c.   Eat healthy. Some lose their appetites during a crisis and others overeat. Avoid either extreme. Force yourself to eat something even if you don't feel hungry. But avoid using food or drink to medicate. Make a point to eat three well balanced meals a day.

d.   Exercise. Go for a walk, ride a bike, or take an exercise class. Physical activity can burn excess adrenaline created by trauma and it releases endorphins which fight depression.

3.   **Mental Health** – The overwhelming stress caused by betrayal can affect your hormonal balance, which can lead to things such as obsessive thinking, irrational behavior, hypersensitivity, hypervigilance, and depression.

a.   Get hormones tested. Make an appointment to have your doctor test your hormone level, especially if you are experiencing any of the above symptoms.

b.   Talk to a therapist. I recommend you only see a Certified Sex Addiction Therapist (CSAT) or someone who is APSATS (The Association of Partners of Sex Addicts Trauma Specialists) trained.

c.   Read recovery materials. Reading about sexual addiction will give you a better understanding of the subject and reassure you this is not your fault. Focus primarily on reading recovery materials written for the betrayed spouse so your primary focus is your own recovery and not your spouse's.

4.   **Emotional Refreshment** – Embarrassment and shame cause people to want to isolate, especially when dealing with the sensitive subject of sexual addiction. It's not usually the kind of thing we discuss over coffee. But you need connection, with others and yourself.

a. Find a safe person to tell. I caution against telling a lot of people and there are many reasons family members are often not the best ones to tell. But you need to find one safe person with whom you can confide.

b. Join a support group. Find an S-Anon group or some other betrayal support group. There is a great benefit in talking with others who are now or have at one time experienced what you are going through.

c. Do something for yourself. It is not uncommon to lose touch with yourself when you are in relationship with an addict. Take some time to read a book, get a pedicure, enjoy a hobby, or anything that refreshes you.

Make time for self-care. It's vital to your healing and you are worth it!

Day Five Assignments

In Day One's assignment, we looked at the story of Elijah running for his life, away from evil Jezebel. We find him in the wilderness, depressed and wanting to die. He hadn't eaten and all he wanted to do was sleep. An angel woke him and gave him something to eat. Elijah ate it and went back to sleep. Today, we read a little more of the story. *"Then the angel of the Lord came again and touched him and said, 'Get up and eat some more, or the journey ahead will be too much for you'"* (1 Kings 19:7 NLT).

Elijah was in the middle of a traumatic time, fleeing for his life. Notice that God sent an angel to do for Elijah what he was not doing for himself. Elijah was neglecting his basic needs. What I find most significant in this passage is the angel's reason for this admonishment; the journey that faced Elijah would overwhelm him if he didn't take care of himself.

Recovery from the trauma caused by betrayal is possible. But it is a long and difficult journey. If you do not make yourself a priority and practice healthy self-care, it will be too much for you and healing becomes unlikely. So follow God's command. Love yourself.

Self-Care

Recovery won't just happen. You must be intentional about pursuing it. This will require adopting a new schedule. I challenge you to incorporate the following into your schedule.

Daily:

1. Pray. Start your day by connecting with God. Ask him to help you heal. End your day by thanking him for helping you through another day and for the progress you have made.
2. Read recovery material. I suggest spending a minimum of 15 minutes on this.
3. Check-in with (call, text, or email) someone regarding your recovery.

4. Practice good self-care. Eat regularly with a focus on a healthy balance. Get plenty of sleep. Go for a walk, ride a bike, take an aerobics class, or do something else for exercise.

Weekly:

1. Participate in at least one support group meeting.
2. Do something for yourself. Get a massage, have lunch with a friend, get a pedicure, take a class, go for a drive, enjoy a hobby, see a movie, or do something else that refreshes you.
3. Attend church.

Monthly:

1. See a therapist or other mental health professional.
2. Take a recovery day. Spend the day at the park or beach, go antiquing, read a good book, go hiking, or do anything else that recharges your battery and refreshes your spirit.

Next Step: Develop your own Recovery Schedule.

WEEK TWO
Safety First

"Your own safety is at stake when your neighbor's wall is ablaze."

\- Horace

Day One
No Place Like Home

When I was growing up, there was a popular children's game called freeze tag. In this game someone was "it." This person chased the other children, attempting to tag one, in which case the tagged person was frozen and couldn't move until someone else unfroze her. The way we played it, there was also a home base, a place where a child could be safe from being tagged. Anywhere away from home base left the child vulnerable to being tagged and frozen, but as long as she was touching home base, she was safe.

In real life, everyone needs a home base where he or she feels safe from the outside world. Ideally, our home with family should be such a place. Unfortunately, when compulsive sexual behavior is present in the home, it usually ceases to feel like a safe place. Being tagged by this leaves the victim feeling somewhat frozen, like in the game, only this is no game and no one is coming to unfreeze her.

Everyday tasks feel overwhelming and an oppressive fog settles in. The discovery of sexual betrayal can cause such trauma that everything that once felt safe is now called into question. This can leave the betrayed party doubting her own reality and her ability to accurately discern who and what is safe.

While this may or may not involve physical safety, it most definitely affects feelings of spiritual, emotional and mental safety. Lies, dishonesty and deception are such a part of an addict's life, it is difficult to find an aspect of the marital home and relationship not adversely impacted. How do you, the wounded spouse, reestablish safety? No matter how remorseful and sincere the offending spouse may look and sound, he cannot be trusted to provide this safety on his own. You must determine what you need to feel safe.

Though there may be some similarities, each person's list will be different. This week we will address some components to consider.

Ultimately, God is the only one who is truly and consistently safe. He will never let you down. Draw close to him.

"You are my hiding place; you will protect me from trouble and surround me with songs of deliverance" (Psalm 32:7).

Day One Assignments

1. When you were growing up, did your home feel like a safe place?
   Yes ☐ No ☐ Explain your answer. _____
   _____
   _____
   _____

2. Prior to discovering your husband's sexual acting out, did you feel
   like your home was a safe place? Yes ☐ No ☐ Explain your answer.
   _____
   _____
   _____
   _____

3. Prior to discovering your husband's sexual acting out, did you feel
   physically and emotionally safe with him? Yes ☐ No ☐ Explain your
   answer. _____
   _____
   _____
   _____

4. Do you feel safe and at peace in your home right now? Yes ☐ No ☐
   Explain your answer. _____
   _____
   _____
   _____

Next Step: Admit to God any lack of peace and safety you are currently
experiencing in your home and in your relationship with your spouse.
Commit to looking to God and trusting him for that each day.

Day Two
You Complete Me

All of us enter marriage with certain expectations. Problems arise when those expectations fail to be met. Certainly, fidelity is a reasonable expectation. But, are there some common expectations of a spouse that are misplaced? In the 1996 film *Jerry Maguire*, Tom Cruise made famous the quote, "You complete me," while speaking to his love interest. Did you enter marriage with the mindset that your spouse completes you? What does that even mean? Is that God's plan for marriage?

Before you can successfully determine what you desire your spouse to do or not do to help you to feel safe in your home at this time, we should take a look at what are reasonable expectations of spouses in general. Is it reasonable to expect our spouses to complete us? The Bible says, *"In Him (Christ) you have been made complete"* (Colossians 2:10 NASB). No man ever has or ever will complete you, even if he has no problem with sexual compulsion. You are made complete in Christ alone.

Is it reasonable to expect a spouse to meet all of your spiritual, physical, mental, and emotional needs? Nowhere in Scripture do we see God instructing the husband, nor any other person, to meet all of those needs. It is simply not possible. The only One who is capable of meeting all of your needs is God. He is not only able, he is willing. *"And my God will meet all your needs according to the riches of his glory in Christ Jesus"* (Philippians 4:19). When we look to others to do for us what only God can do, we become like a beggar, holding out an empty cup to passersby.

At this point, it may be hard to believe that there could be anything good about discovering you are married to someone with a porn or sex addiction. But if you are like most, in time you will come to see a number of positives emerge during your healing journey. One of the greatest blessings that can come from betrayal trauma is the realization that we have expected others to provide for us that which only God can provide, and consequently we begin looking to him to meet our needs. I've found that when I come to God each day, asking him to fill me up with himself, I begin to see that which I receive from others as just part of the overflow. It is like icing on the cake.

Day Two Assignments

1. Did you enter into marriage with any expectations you now realize were unrealistic? If so, what were they? _____

   _____

   _____

   _____

   _____

2. In the past, how have you depended on your spouse to provide you with feelings of security?

   Spiritually? _____

   _____

   _____

   _____

   Emotionally? _____

   _____

   _____

   _____

   Financially? _____

   _____

   _____

   _____

   Physically? _____

   _____

   _____

   _____

   Mentally? _____

   _____

   _____

   _____

3. Have you trusted in your spouse more than God to provide you with a sense of safety and security? If so, in what way? _____

_____

_____

_____

_____

Next Step: Confess to God any way in which you have placed your trust in your spouse over him to provide you with a sense of safety and security. Commit to trusting him daily to provide for your spiritual, physical, emotional, and mental needs.

Day Three
Not There for Me

The trauma of betrayal can leave the wife shattered and desperate to know that her whole marriage isn't a lie; longing to see contrition in her husband; yearning to be comforted; hoping to feel safe again in her marriage. To the logical mind, it seems that the offending husband who is serious about saving his marriage would be eager and willing to meet those needs and more. But is that reasonable?

It is important to know that dealing with a sex addict who is in early recovery is much like dealing with an adolescent. His emotional growth is stunted, he is typically self-absorbed and he has limited capacity for empathy. According to some experts, it takes at least ninety days of recovery and sobriety for the addict's brain and thinking to clear enough that he begins to grasp the weight of his sin and he begins to feel the depths of the pain he has caused.

What does this mean for the wounded spouse? It means that expecting her husband to be there for her emotionally will likely lead to further heartache. This deficiency on the part of the husband is not necessarily indicative of a lack of desire to get well or to make the marriage work.

This does not release the husband of any responsibility for the healing process. (Tomorrow, we will look at what can be expected of him.) But it does mean that the betrayed spouse will likely need to look to have her emotional needs met primarily in some other way during this time. As we read on Day Two, God is faithful to supply our needs. It is important to turn to him and ask him to meet that need.

God can work through various ways to meet your emotional needs during this difficult time when your spouse is unable to offer the emotional support you need and crave. This may be achieved through the caring words of a trusted friend, the prayers of your clergy, the companionship of your pet, in addition to the peace of God's abiding presence in your life. Let go of your predetermined mindset of what that emotional support should look like and surrender to God's plan to provide it for you in this season.

Day Three Assignments

"God is our refuge and strength, an ever-present help in trouble" (Psalm 46:1).

1. Have you experienced a lack of emotional support from your spouse? Yes □ No □ If so, how does that make you feel? _____

    _____

    _____

    _____

2. Have you interpreted any deficit in your husband's emotional availability as a lack of commitment to recovery or the marriage? Yes □ No □

3. How does learning that an addict in early recovery usually lacks the ability to adequately show empathy and other emotions, make you feel? Does it give you any comfort? Does it cause you to feel angry or hopeless? Explain your response. _____

    _____

    _____

    _____

4. In what other ways have you experienced emotional support during this time? _____

    _____

    _____

    _____

Next Step: Ask God to give you a better understanding of your spouse's limited ability, at this time, to give you the emotional support you need. Ask God to meet that need and then trust him to do so.

Day Four
The Comfort Zone

As we saw on Day Three, someone in early recovery from porn and sex addiction is usually unable to provide all of the comfort and empathy the wounded spouse desperately needs. However, there are some changes the recovering addict can make that will help restore a sense of peace and safety for the one suffering the betrayal trauma. It is important for the wounded spouse to consider what those things are and to communicate those to her husband.

If you've discovered that your spouse has struggled on any level with compulsive sexual behavior, I strongly suggest that you get tested for STDs and refrain from any unprotected sex with him until he has done the same and you have seen the results. This is a good place to start with your safety list. Regardless of any insistence that he may have that such tests are not necessary because he has not crossed certain lines that would put either of you at risk, pursue testing. Addicts are notorious for deception and when your health is at stake, this is not the time to start taking their word for it.

Beyond that, what other things are causing you to feel unsafe at this time? If your husband has had any partners, it will be difficult for you both to move forward with healing if he has any further contact with such persons. Deleting cell numbers and social media contacts is a good place to start.

Consider what you desire regarding your physical space. Do you want him to be out of the home temporarily, or at least out of the bedroom? What about any physical touch at this point?

If there has been pornography viewed in your home, are there blocks or accountability programs you'd like to have on devices? Would you feel more comfortable if your spouse gave you passcodes and access to all of his devices and accounts? If money has been spent as a part of his acting out, are there any safeguards you'd like in place regarding his carrying cash? Do you have access to all bank accounts?

As has been previously stated, the words of an addict aren't usually trustworthy. What recovery steps would you like to see him take that would help you to believe he is serious about breaking free from his past destructive behaviors? Do you want him to see a CSAT, attend 12-step meetings, have an accountability partner, or do a therapeutic disclosure with a polygraph?

These are just some of the things to consider when developing a safety plan. Take some time to think and pray about it. Keep in mind, there may be things that come up later that you did not think of originally. In that case, you can add to your plan. Also, as you both progress in recovery, you may feel some things on your list are no longer issues for you. Tomorrow, we will look at how to communicate your plan to your spouse.

Day Four Assignments

As was mentioned earlier, not everyone's safety plan will look the same. Take some time now to write down some things you would like your husband to do or not do that you think will promote feelings of peace and safety in you.

I've included the following list to spur your thinking.

- STD testing
- Delete certain numbers
- Grant access to all accounts
- Move out
- No physical contact
- Attend 12-step meetings
- Get a sponsor
- Porn blockers
- Do a therapeutic disclosure
- No phone at night
- Report whereabouts
- Attend church
- Do recovery exercises
- Limit alcohol
- Eliminate contact with acting partners
- Delete social media accounts
- Share pass codes
- Move to guest room
- Limit cash on hand
- See a CSAT
- Covenant Eyes
- Have an accountability partner
- Take a polygraph
- No computer use alone
- Have an out of town plan
- No time alone with females
- Read recovery materials
- Avoid bars & clubs unless you're there

Your list may include more or less than ten. I've given you a few sentence starters.

1. I would like you to _____

2. I would prefer you not _____

3. I'd feel more comfortable if _____

4. I will not stay in relationship with someone who _____
    _____

5. _____

6. _____

7. _____

8. _____

9. _____

10. _____

Next Step: Use your answers as a starting place to create your own safety plan. Continue to seek God's direction and revisit your list over a period of several days before finalizing it.

Day Five
Speak Up

"You covet and cannot obtain, so you fight and quarrel. You do not have, because you do not ask. You ask and do not receive, because you ask wrongly" (James 4:2-3 ESV).

Too often we expect others to read our minds, so we fail to speak up for what we need. In the Book of James, God, through the author James, the brother of Jesus, gives us sound principles for asking for what we need in all areas of our lives. The word "covet" means to yearn to have or possess. How many times has your desperate need for safety caused conflict with your spouse? Have you clearly expressed how he might meet that desire?

Hopefully you have developed a list, either previously or during yesterday's assignment, of what you think would help you to feel a sense of safety and security in your present circumstances. Before you ask for what you need, assess your motive for each request. Is this something you truly think will aid you in achieving feelings of security? Or is this request an attempt to control or punish the other person? Lamentations 3:40 says, *"Let us examine our ways and test them, and let us return to the Lord."* Ask God to help you clarify your motives.

Once you have done that and have made any adjustments to your list (and your attitude), then you are ready to approach the person and ask for what you want. Timing and demeanor are critically important. Use wisdom regarding when to broach the subject. Avoid a time when either of you will be rushed or when there is already an issue of conflict. When you do proceed, do so with humility and grace. *"Let your speech always be gracious, seasoned with salt, so that you may know how you ought to answer each person"* (Colossians 4:6 ESV).

You have been terribly wounded and it is understandable that you might be tempted to present the items on your list as demands. It is important to remember that you cannot make another person do what you want them to do. However, you can ask for what you think you need and you can state clearly which, if any of those items, are absolutely critical for you to remain in the relationship. For instance, it is understandable and wise to make clear that discontinuing all contact with any person with whom your spouse has acted out is a nonnegotiable. Unfortunately, you should have a plan in place if he refuses or agrees and then doesn't follow through.

Finally, as much as you may think having your spouse fulfill all of the items listed on your safety plan will provide you with a sense of security and peace, that may not be the end result, or at least not to the degree that you'd like. It is possible for you to achieve a sense of peace, safety and security regardless of your spouse's choices. So while it can certainly be helpful to your healing to have a spouse who is willing to accommodate your list of desires, you will likely soon recognize that situations will continue to arise that can threaten your feelings of safety because there are no guarantees that your spouse will remain faithful in all circumstances. If an addict wants to act out, he will find another way and no amount of parameters will prevent that.

The passage from James that we saw at the beginning of this lesson most definitely applies to our relationship with God. Ultimately, our sense of safety and security rests in God alone. Ask him to provide that for you. Only then will you cease to be at the mercy of others' choices.

Day Five Assignments

1. Have you previously experienced conflict and quarreling over situations you have listed in your safety plan? Yes☐ No ☐

2. Have you previously asked specifically for your husband to make changes to accommodate your needs for emotional, physical, or spiritual safety? Yes ☐ No ☐ If yes, briefly explain. _____

_____

_____

_____

_____

3. Have you assessed the motives behind the items listed on your safety plan? Yes ☐ No ☐ If not, take the time to examine your list and ask God to show you any items that stem from wrong motives. Does it contain any requests that are designed to control or punish your spouse?
Yes ☐ No ☐ How might you need to adjust your list? _____

_____

_____

_____

4. Have you experienced feelings of insecurity despite your husband's efforts to do things to help facilitate a sense of safety for you?
Yes ☐ No ☐ Explain your answer. _____

_____

_____

_____

5. Do you have any items on your list that you consider nonnegotiable?
Yes ☐ No ☐ If yes, do you have a plan in place if your husband refuses to agree to that request, or agrees to it but fails to follow through?
Yes ☐ No ☐ If yes, what is that item and what is your plan? _____

_____

_____

_____

_____

6. Do you believe you can feel safe and secure regardless of your circumstances or another's choices? Yes ☐ No ☐ If no, ask God to provide that sense of peace and safety and then trust him to do so. If you do believe it is possible but you haven't been experiencing it, have you recently asked God to provide it for you? Yes ☐ No ☐ The Bible says to ask and keep asking.

Next Step: Consider your motive for each item on your plan and make any needed adjustments. Ask a sponsor or counselor to read it and give you feedback. Present it to your spouse at an appropriate time.

WEEK THREE
Triggers

*"We are not a victim of our emotions or thoughts.
We can understand our triggers and use them
as tools to help us respond more objectively."*

\- Elizabeth Thornton

Day One
Definition and Explanation

God has created the brain as a highly complex and fascinating organ in the way it assesses a threat, responds and files the memory. This process is crucial for survival. As an example, you see a man in a blue shirt approaching with a gun. Immediately, the brain begins processing this information and sending signals to the rest of the body. If the brain perceives this as a threat, then automatically the body will respond with a rush of adrenaline initiating such responses as a racing heart, sweating, and a knot in the stomach. These are a part of the body's fight, flight, or freeze responses. The body amps up to run away from the threat, fight back, or freeze to avoid detection.

If the man proceeds to rob you, your brain will store this memory with both conscious and subconscious memories of the event. In the future, if you see someone with a gun, your brain will check your database and once again engage the threat response sequence. Unfortunately, the brain will link neutral information with the threat. For example, you may be walking down the street and see a man in a blue shirt and your brain will retrieve the memory of the robbery and engage the same threat response sequence even though there is no threat. However, you will likely react with the same physiological and emotional responses as if it were a real threat.

This same kind of process happens with the memories associated with the discovery of a spouse's sexual acting out. For example, let's say you were in the grocery store when you received a text from a woman confessing she has been having an affair with your husband. Your brain perceives a threat to your marriage and family and sends signals to the body to respond accordingly. Even though you aren't physically in immediate danger, your body will likely respond with tight muscles, racing heart, sweating and other physiological responses. This memory will be stored with both relevant and neutral information.

A trigger is something that cues or sets off physical and/or emotional response in the body and draws you back to a past experience or memory. The trigger can be a conscious memory such as a text from the same number or it can be an unconscious connection of the smell in the produce section in which you were standing when you received the text or a song that happened to be playing over the speakers in the store at that time.

Dealing with triggers can be one of the most difficult aspects of recovery. Many of the immediate reactions include fear, emotional outbursts, uncontrollable crying, anxiety attacks, and lashing out. Learning to identify your triggers and conditioning yourself to respond in healthy and productive ways are vital to recovering your peace and serenity. This week we will begin the work of identifying your triggers and developing a plan to avoid, prepare for, and manage them.

You are not responsible for the trauma that caused your triggers. But you are responsible for how you respond to them.

Triggers explain but don't excuse behavior.

Day One Assignments

Russian scientist Ivan Pavlov is well known for his experiments in which dogs were fed when a bell was rung. The natural response to encountering the food was for the dogs to salivate. But through repeated conditioning, he went on to prove that eventually the dogs would begin to salivate at the mere ringing of the bell even if no food was presented. The bell was a neutral cue. It had no inherent scientific significance.

Similarly, many of the triggers we encounter due to betrayal trauma are neutral cues that just happened to be linked in our memories to the discovery of that betrayal. There are others that are directly linked. Either way, learning to recondition our brains to lessen and hopefully eliminate the effects of these triggers is a key component of recovery.

We can't necessarily control what triggers we encounter, but we can learn to change how we respond to them. God's Word tells us this is possible. *"Do not conform to the pattern of this world, but be transformed by the renewing of your mind"* (Romans 12:2). We will discover this week how we can begin that renewal process.

Questions

1. Have you found yourself triggered by sights, sounds, or smells that have evoked strong emotions or physical symptoms reminiscent of your discovery of some aspect of your husband's betrayal? How have you responded? _____

   _____

   _____

   _____

   _____

   _____

2. Have you reacted to triggers by yelling, shaming, blaming, shunning, or in some other way attempting to punish your spouse and justified it as being deserved? If so, how did you feel afterward? _____

_____

_____

_____

_____

3. Are you honestly ready to learn how to respond to triggers in a healthy way without lashing out at your spouse? Why or why not? _____

_____

_____

_____

_____

Next Step: Commit to learning how to respond in a healthy way to triggers. Ask God to begin renewing your mind.

Day Two
Identifying Triggers

Life can feel like a minefield after the discovery of sexual betrayal. Everywhere you go and everything you see can seem to be a reminder of the hurt that you have experienced. Your mind may be flooded with intrusive thoughts and images. These are triggers and they can come internally and externally. Today, we will break these down and consider a number of examples so you may be better equipped to recognize the triggers in your own life.

Internal Triggers – A thought, emotion, or feeling inside your body

Examples:
- Memories
- Thoughts
- Feeling anxious
- Feeling like you have a pit in your stomach
- Feeling unattractive
- Feeling unappreciated
- Loneliness
- Feeling out of control
- Sadness

External Triggers – Involve your senses (sight, sound, smell, touch)

Examples:

Places
- Favorite restaurant
- Past vacation spot
- Location where you learned of betrayal
- A location where spouse acted out or similar place
- Beach, Victoria's Secret or place with scantily clad women or mannequins

People
- Someone who is your spouse's type
- Former or current acting out partner
- Woman dressed provocatively
- Someone who looks like former partner

Things
- Certain smell
- Love song, break-up song or favorite song as a couple
- Photograph
- Past gift with a special meaning
- Text or call
- Husband working late
- Out of town business trip
- A name or number on a piece of paper
- An anniversary

Day Two Assignments

In the story of Peter's denial of Christ, Jesus had prophesied that all of his disciples would fall away on the night of his betrayal. Peter vowed he would never fall away, even if everyone else did. Jesus responded, *"This very night, before the rooster crows, you will disown me three times"* (Matthew 26:34). Later that night, after Jesus' arrest, Peter denied knowing Christ three times. Upon the third time, the Bible says, *"Immediately a rooster crowed. Then Peter remembered the word Jesus had spoken...And he went outside and wept bitterly"* (Matthew 26:75).

The crow of the rooster triggered Peter's memory and he was overcome with emotion. Similarly, there are things that remind us of our spouses' betrayal that evoke strong responses. Those triggers can come from within us, such as a thought, feeling, or memory, or they can be external, such as a place, person or thing. The first step to learning to deal with these in a healthy way is identifying what triggers you.

Unfortunately, we can experience a trigger, begin feeling anxious, angry, or sad, yet not make the connection. I've found it helpful to pray for wisdom and discernment in this area. *"If any of you lacks wisdom, you should ask God, who gives generously to all without finding fault, and it will be given to you"* (James 1:5). When you suddenly feel a wave of emotion come over you, stop and consider where you just were, what was going on around you, or what you were just thinking about. Quite possibly, your change in mood was the result of a trigger.

1. Identify and write down as many of your internal triggers that come to mind. _____

   _____

   _____

   _____

   _____

   _____

   _____

2. Identify and write down as many of your external triggers that come to mind. _____

_____
_____
_____
_____
_____
_____
_____
_____

Next Step: Ask God to give you the wisdom and discernment to identify those things that trigger you and ask him to equip you to deal with them in a way that honors him.

Day Three
Avoiding Triggers

"The wise are cautious and avoid danger; fools plunge ahead with reckless confidence" (Proverbs 14:16 NLT).

Triggers can derail your recovery progress in an instant. One of the wisest things you can do in early recovery is to avoid triggers whenever possible. This will likely involve times you need to speak up and set boundaries. Here are two types of boundaries for dealing with triggers:

Boundaries you set for yourself.

- Avoid driving by sexually oriented businesses.
- Avoid driving by places your husband has acted out.
- Avoid watching movies or TV shows with scenes of infidelity, nudity, or sexual acts.
- Avoid listening to music with depressing lyrics or special songs that now cause triggers.
- Avoid lingerie stores, catalogs, and magazines.
- Avoid the news.
- Avoid people who trigger you.
- Avoid looking at photo albums.

Boundaries you request of your husband.

- Avoid any areas where he's acted out.
- Have no contact with any former acting out partners.
- Avoid being alone with any women.
- Avoid carrying cash.
- Avoid working late whenever possible.
- Avoid time on computer in separate room while at home.
- Take no trips to the pool or beach.

These are just a few of the ways triggers can possibly be avoided. Many of these will be temporary until you and/or your spouse are further along in recovery and less apt to be triggered by such things. There are others that you are always wise in attempting to avoid. Unfortunately, many triggers cannot be avoided and tomorrow we will begin preparing for how to deal with those.

Day Three Assignments

"Give careful thought to the paths for your feet and be steadfast in all your ways" (Proverbs 4:26).

Triggers are the unfortunate reminders of the betrayal you've experienced. The pain caused by betrayal can feel suffocating and anything that cues that memory can feel like you're having more dirt poured in on you, choking out what little oxygen you have remaining. Unfortunately, many triggers are beyond our control. You would be wise, especially in early recovery, to avoid those you can.

A. Make a list of known triggers that you can reasonably avoid.

1. _____
2. _____
3. _____
4. _____
5. _____
6. _____
7. _____
8. _____
9. _____
10. _____

B. Make a list of things your husband does or doesn't do that trigger you and which you can request he avoid.

1. _____
2. _____
3. _____
4. _____
5. _____

6. _____

7. _____

8. _____

9. _____

10. _____

Next Step: Ask God to help you to be alert and watchful for the traps the enemy will set for you by way of triggers, and to give you the wisdom on how to avoid them whenever possible.

Day Four
Preparing for Triggers

When a trigger hits, it can have such an overwhelming impact that it can be difficult to think clearly in the moment. Your best chance at successfully battling that attack is to prepare in advance. Imagine the catastrophe that would result if the commander of an army waited until the enemy attacked to begin training and arming his troops. How can you prepare for the inevitable triggers you'll encounter?

1. Practice good self-care.

One of the best ways to avoid overreacting to a trigger is to be in a healthy place spiritually, mentally, emotionally, and physically when you encounter it. Start each day by connecting with God. Don't isolate. Stay connected with friends. Take the time to do things for yourself. Get plenty of rest, exercise and eat right. Remember the acronym, HALT. This stands for hungry, angry, lonely, and tired. Any of these conditions can cause you to be more susceptible to internal triggers, more vulnerable to external triggers and powerless over either.

2. Develop a plan.

Developing a strategy in advance for dealing with triggers, better positions you for success in the inevitable battle with them. A good plan is to start each day asking God to help you to respond to whatever triggers you may face that day in a healthy way that honors him. Writing out scripture or encouraging quotes on an index card gives you a weapon to access in the fight against triggers. Making a list of things about your spouse for which you are grateful can also be useful. It would be a good idea to either commit these things to memory or to carry those cards and lists with you so you can read them when you are feeling overwhelmed by a trigger. Finally, it is wise to have in mind the name of someone you can call or text when you are feeling triggered. Letting that person know in advance of your intentions will make them more likely to respond quickly when you do reach out. Most importantly, don't forget to make that call.

Though it is unlikely you will make it through this healing journey without repeatedly encountering triggers, you don't have to let them wreck your day or sidetrack your recovery progress. By practicing good self-care and developing a plan in advance, you will be prepared to face those triggers victoriously.

Day Four Assignments

"Finally, be strong in the Lord and in his mighty power. Put on the full armor of God, so that you can take your stand against the devil's schemes. For our struggle is not against flesh and blood, but against the rulers, against the authorities, against the powers of this dark world and against the spiritual forces of evil in the heavenly realms" (Ephesians 6:10-12).

When discovering your spouse has betrayed you, it is easy to see him as your enemy and forget that sex addicts are sick people, not bad people. The real enemy is Satan, whom the Bible compares to a roaring lion seeking prey to devour. He wants to destroy you, your spouse, your marriage, and your family. One of his tactics is to do everything he can to remind you of how much your spouse has hurt you.

The time to determine how to handle those reminders, those triggers when they come, is before they do. Take steps now to prepare. Recognize that you are more vulnerable for an intense reaction to them when you haven't been taking care of yourself and you are worn out. Remember the acronym, HALT: hungry, angry, lonely, and tired. The enemy doesn't fight fair. He will seize upon the opportunity to attack when you are weak, just as a lion looks for the wounded and isolated gazelle. Practice self-care.

Prepare your mind for battle by filling it with scripture, encouraging words, and gratitude. Write those things out on index cards and keep them close by to read when a trigger hits. And decide now who you can call when that time comes. Choose someone who is wise and who is willing to help you walk through it.

Benjamin Franklin said, "By failing to prepare, you are preparing to fail."

1. List one thing you will do this week for self-care. _____

_____

_____

2. Write down at least one scripture or encouraging statement that you can read when a trigger hits. Example: "I can do all things through Christ who gives me strength" (Philippians 4:13); Storms don't last forever, but strong people do. _____

   _____

   _____

3. List three things about your husband for which you are grateful.

   _____

   _____

   _____

4. Write down the name of the person you will call when you are triggered. _____

"The horse is made ready for the day of battle, but the victory rests with the Lord" (Proverbs 21:31).

Next Step: Prepare for triggers and then pray for God to give you victory in the battle.

Day Five
Managing Triggers

Despite our best efforts, we cannot avoid all triggers. Today we take a look at some useful tools for navigating our way through the tumultuous waters of triggers without capsizing. Just as you wouldn't go white water rafting without advance preparation, hopefully you are not encountering your triggers without some of the planning we covered on Day Four. Strap on that helmet and let's go.

When confronted with a trigger, the body responds much like it did during the original crisis. The sympathetic nervous system is activated from the sudden release of hormones. Symptoms include elevated heart and breathing rate, tightening of the muscles, and sweating. The brain basically goes off-line as the body prepares for action, impairing reasoning, and judgment. Dissociative symptoms such as the feeling that time is slowing down or that what is happening is not real, make it difficult to stay grounded and present. The first line of defense is to slow the body's crisis response. To facilitate this:

1. **Take deep breaths and focus on relaxing your muscles and slowing your heart rate.**

2. **Get grounded, return to the present and reconnect with your surroundings by identifying three things you can see, and/or by touching a few things around you.**

Sometimes the trigger is obvious. Other times, your body and emotions recognize and respond to the trigger before you are aware of it. In either case, the trigger signals an area that needs attention and healing. It might not be possible to adequately address the trigger at that time. It is an important part of your recovery journey to take the time, at some point, to revisit the issue.

3. **Identify and process the trigger.**

Since sound reasoning can be impaired by encountering a trigger, it is not uncommon for negative thoughts to run rampant. This can lead to such feelings as inadequacy, victimization, and anger at spouse or self. This is the time to pull out your lists of scripture, encouraging statements, and gratitude.

4. **Engage in healthy self-talk.**

The trigger interrupts your thoughts and actions. The enemy of your soul wants to take this opportunity to hijack your thoughts and send you plunging over the falls to destruction. Take control. What were you doing before you encountered the trigger?

5. **Refocus.**

If your attempts to refocus are unsuccessful, try something else.

6. **Distract yourself by going for a walk, singing a song, cleaning out a closet, or doing anything that will take your mind off of what is triggering you.**

Finally, it helps to talk it through.

7. **Call someone.**

Triggers can be debilitating if not managed in a healthy way. Remember, triggers can elicit the same feelings and emotions as the original crisis, but they are not the same.

Recognize a trigger is not the same as the original trauma.

8. **Show yourself grace.**

You have experienced great trauma and it takes intensive work and a good deal of time for your body and mind to stabilize enough that you can become consistently successful in dealing with triggers. When you don't handle a trigger as well as you would have liked, be kind to yourself. Don't beat yourself up or become discouraged. Keep using your tools and working toward healing. You will get better.

Day Five Assignments

Ensure that you have prepared for triggers. Keep a journal of any encounters you have with triggers this week. Evaluate how well you did at handling them.

1. Did you recognize the trigger as such when it was happening? Yes □ No □

2. Did you attempt to slow the physical crisis response by slowing down your breathing and relaxing your muscles? Yes □ No □ If so, did that help? Explain _____ _____ _____

3. Did you attempt to stay present and grounded using the tools discussed on Day 4? Yes □ No □

4. Did negative thoughts flood your mind? If so, did you combat them with scripture, positive sayings, or by recalling things about your spouse for which you are grateful? Yes □ No □

5. Were you able to refocus and return to what you were doing prior to the trigger, before much time passed? Yes □ No □

6. Did you do anything to distract yourself from what was triggering you? If so, what did you do and did it help? _____ _____

7. Did you call someone? Yes □ No □

8. Do you feel like you better handled triggers this week than you did before this week's lessons? Yes □ No □

9. How can you better prepare for future triggers? _____ _____ _____

Next Step: Ask God to give you wisdom as you assess your progress in addressing triggers and as you determine what, if any, adjustments you need to make.

WEEK FOUR
Control

*"One of the most rewarding and important moments
in life is the moment you finally find the
courage to let go of what you can't change."*

\- Marc Chernoff

Day One
The Power of Control

One of the most comforting pieces of information learned by betrayed spouses is that they did nothing to cause their husband's addiction. But that is usually coupled with the fact that there is nothing they can do to control it either. The knowledge that she has no power to direct her husband's behavior or the course of his recovery can leave the wounded spouse feeling helpless.

Psychologist Elliot D. Cohen calls losing control "one of the most prevalent fears" people have. This fear, Cohen says, is "that if you don't manage to control the outcome of future events, something terrible will happen." I believe that is precisely the thinking behind the hurting wife's attempt to control her addicted spouse. It is a natural defense mechanism to try to do whatever it takes to avoid further pain.

Even with the knowledge that she has no power to control her spouse, it is not uncommon for the wife to use covert tactics to attempt it anyway. Often it is done in such subtle ways, she is not aware she is doing it. She might use anger, shame, sarcasm, criticism, pouting, the silent treatment, or withholding love, sex, praise or affection to control the addict. She might swing to the other extreme and shower her husband with attention, kindness, and praise or be sexual with him or avoid addressing her own hurts and needs, or making him uncomfortable in any way, in an attempt to keep him from acting out.

Efforts to control a porn or sex addict are futile and exhausting. But the need to find safety in power and control is a natural reaction to deep mistrust caused by betrayal. The Bible has a lot to say about being self-controlled but nothing to say about controlling someone else. We will enjoy more peace when we accept our limitations and focus on the one person we can control – ourselves.

Day One Assignments

1. Have you been the one to research recovery materials and meetings for your spouse or schedule his therapy appointments? Yes □ No □

2. Have you used the silent treatment, pouting, sarcasm, insults, anger, blaming, or belittling to try to effect change in your spouse?
Yes □ No □

3. Have you withheld affection, sex, or praise to control your spouse?
Yes □ No □

4. Have you been sexual with your spouse in hopes it will keep him from acting out? Yes □ No □

5. Have you withheld your feelings, concerns, or needs from your spouse because you didn't want to cause him stress or discomfort, thinking that might cause a slip? Yes □ No □

6. In what ways have you attempted to control your spouse? _____
_____
_____
_____
_____
_____

7. Do you accept that you cannot control your spouse, his recovery, or his sobriety? Yes □ No □

8. How does it make you feel to know that you cannot do anything to control whether or not your spouse acts out? _____
_____
_____
_____
_____

Next Step: Ask God to reveal to you any means you've used in an attempt to control your spouse or his recovery. Ask him to help you accept your inability to control anyone other than yourself and to help you focus on your own healing.

Day Two
Why We Try to Control Others

It is unlikely that anyone would welcome the label of control freak. But being in a relationship with a porn or sex addict can easily lead someone to grasp for every bit of control possible. Why? There can be many reasons for the desire to control.

One thing that can lead to controlling behaviors is a feeling of pride or superiority, especially when married to someone who is sexually broken and has sinned as a result. The focus becomes the flaws, shortcomings, and sickness of the addict, leading the wife to believe he's bad and she's good; therefore, she knows best what he needs to be "fixed."

The need for security is another reason people can become obsessed with control. When a woman discovers that she is married to someone with a sexual addiction, she can feel her world has been turned upside down, resulting in great anxiety. In an attempt to regain feelings of safety and stability in her life, she may attempt to control her husband's every move. Unfortunately, this usually leads to more anxiety.

When someone recognizes one area of his or her life is out of control, it can lead to hyper control in other areas. This is easily seen in the betrayed wife who becomes obsessed with cleaning and organizing or orchestrating the lives of her children or others. She desperately wants to feel like there is something in her life over which she does have control.

Fear of abandonment can lead to a need to control. If she can control another's life, that person will be dependent on her and won't leave. Rarely does she recognize the correlation.

Emotions such as fear, sadness, or helplessness can result from betrayal. But this can leave the victim feeling vulnerable and weak. To avoid appearing as such, the individual will exert control and power in an attempt to show strength. Or rather than attempting to appear strong to others, the individual may use control to suppress those distressing emotions in herself. In either case, control is the mask for undesired emotions.

Finally, lack of trust can lead someone to become controlling. In the case of infidelity, the lack of trust in the betraying spouse is understandable. But it also demonstrates a lack of trust in God's ability or willingness to work all things, even bad things, for good.

Regardless of the reasons behind the desire to be in control, the attempts come at a great cost. Tomorrow we will look at those costs.

Day Two Assignments

When my son was little, everything in his room had a place. There were colored baskets in his closet and each toy had an assigned colored basket. This all seemed quite logical to me. When my son had finished playing with a toy, he was to put it away in the correct basket before removing another toy. One day, as a friend was over to play, I heard my son yelling at his friend because the friend had put a toy in the "wrong" basket. I suddenly felt great guilt as I realized my obsessiveness with control had caused my son such anxiety that he was berating a friend for not doing things the "correct" way.

Why had I become such a control freak? I did not know at the time that my husband was a sex addict. But I did know something wasn't right in our relationship and I had been unable to do anything to change the situation and restore order and harmony to my household. So, oblivious to the reason why, I set out to control everything in my life and household possible, including my innocent son, in an attempt to counter the out of control feeling I had about my marriage.

1. Have you recognized in your own life a tendency to be controlling? Have others accused you of being controlling? If so, take some time to consider what might be behind that behavior.

2. Do you often believe you know the correct or best way to accomplish a task? Yes □ No □

3. At times, do you consider others to be a distraction to the more important things you are trying to accomplish? Do you think what they are doing is less important? Yes □ No □

4. Do you feel like you can secure a better outcome for your future if you control the people and circumstances around you? Yes □ No □

5. Do you find yourself obsessed with organizing and cleaning? Yes □ No □

6. Do you find yourself doing things for others that they can do for themselves? Yes □ No □

7. Do you consider emotions such as fear, sadness, and helplessness to convey weakness or vulnerability? Yes □ No □

8. Are you skeptical about people's motives or intentions? Yes □ No □

9. Do you believe that God can take the worst circumstances in your life and make something good come from them? Yes □ No □

Next Step: Ask God to make you more aware of times when you are being controlling. Take the time to consider what emotion or thinking is behind it.

Day Three
The Problem with Control

The desire to be in control goes as far back as the beginning of man. The Bible is full of stories of man attempting to do things to become like God so he could be in control of his own life with no need to depend on God. It has never worked out well, yet that hasn't stopped us from trying. Aside from the obvious fact that God is God and we are not, what is wrong with trying to be in control?

1. It is frustrating.

Attempting to control anything or anyone other than ourselves can be extremely frustrating. Have you ever tried to get a toddler having a meltdown to follow your orders? Or have you tried to get a cat to follow your directions? You may have more success parting the Red Sea than clearing a way through stalled traffic when you're late for an appointment. The reality is most things are out of our control and efforts dismissive of that fact usually rob us of our peace of mind.

2. It leads to a critical spirit.

The pride behind our attempts to control often produce a critical spirit within us. When we think we know best, our way is right, and others are flawed and sinful, we become judgmental. We doubt others' abilities. *"Do not judge, or you too will be judged"* (Matthew 7:1). There are none of us who are righteous (Romans 3:10). We are all flawed and sinful creatures who still have much to learn and room to grow.

3. It causes conflict.

The natural response when we feel someone is attempting to control us is resistance. We have a West Highland White Terrier. She is adorable but she is a terrier, which means she is prone to stubbornness. When I am walking her, as long as I leave slack in the leash, she does pretty well. But if I attempt to pull in one direction, she will immediately pull in the opposite direction. As humans, we typically respond in like manner if we think someone is trying to control us, and conflict ensues.

4. It is exhausting.

Let's be honest. Controlling ourselves is a full-time job. When we add to that trying to orchestrate the schedules, choices, and behaviors of others, it is overwhelming. We may think that we are doing them a favor or being helpful, or we may be trying to prevent them from doing things that negatively affect us. Regardless of the reason, we are taking on a role that is not ours and we are bearing a load that is not ours to bear.

5. It is an illusion.

Whether it is Magic Kingdom's Tomorrowland Speedway Car Ride or Epcot's Test Track, children and adults alike will stand in line for hours for the chance to "drive" those cars. But with both rides, the reality is the cars are on a track and turning the steering wheel makes no difference. It is just an illusion but we enjoy it anyway. So it is with the control of circumstances or people. Our attempts may make us feel better, but our effect is minimal.

It does not matter if it is the sexaholic in our lives, someone else, circumstances, or our surroundings; our efforts to control anything or anyone other than ourselves often lead to frustration, a critical spirit, conflict, exhaustion, and disillusionment. Tomorrow we will count the cost of control.

Day Three Assignments

It is human nature to want to be in control. Therefore, it is our nature to balk at others attempts to control us. As we discovered previously, being in or having been in a relationship with someone who has a sexual addiction can make us feel completely out of control. As a result, it is common for the betrayed spouse to grasp for control of the people and circumstances in her life in effort to reestablish a sense of stability. This is especially true as it relates to the addict and his recovery. As we just read, there are many problems with this. In your own life, what problems have you experienced as a result of your attempts to control anything other than yourself?

1. Have you experienced frustration when trying to control people, circumstances, or outcomes in your life? If so, please explain. _____
   _____
   _____
   _____

2. Do you feel the need to correct people or point out when they are wrong? Do you believe that if something is going to be done right, you have to do it? Do you have difficulty admitting when you are wrong? If these describe you, you may have a critical spirit.

3. Have you experienced relational conflict as a result of trying to tell others what they should or shouldn't do? If so, please explain. _____
   _____
   _____
   _____

4. Have you felt overwhelmed and exhausted from trying to manage another's life in addition to your own? Have you felt resentful because you were taking on someone else's responsibilities? If so, please explain. _____
   _____
   _____
   _____

Next Step: Ask God to use the areas of discomfort in your life to help you determine if any are the result of you trying to control things over which you have no control.

Day Four
The Cost of Control

Actions have consequences. We get to choose our actions but we don't get to choose the consequences. On Day Three, we explored some of the problems with attempting to control people and situations in our lives. Even knowing these, we may still proceed with our attempts at control. But before we do, let's look at what it will cost us. Scripture cautions us to count the cost of something before we undertake it (Luke 14:28). So, what will our efforts to control other people and circumstances cost us?

1. Peace

"What causes fights and quarrels among you? Don't they come from your desires that battle within you? You desire but do not have, so you kill. You covet but you cannot get what you want, so you quarrel and fight" (James 4:1-2). The vast majority of people will resist and refuse others' attempts to control them, leading to conflict and frustration which result in a loss of peace for the one asserting control. Instead of peace there is turmoil, without and within.

2. Joy

It is difficult to relax and enjoy the present when you are focused on insulating yourself from future pain by controlling someone else's choices and behavior to achieve that goal. Rejoice in another's right choices today instead of trying to prevent him from making poor choices tomorrow.

3. Freedom

When you release others to run their own lives and make their own choices, you free up your time and energy to focus on what you can do to produce a healthier you. Your attitude and choices are the only things you can control.

4. Physical & Mental Health

The anxiety that results from the futility of efforts to control another adversely affects your physical and mental well-being. There is an abundance of empirical data on the harmful effects of anxiety and stress on a person. Don't jeopardize your health for a lost cause.

5. Sense of Reality

As we saw yesterday, control is an illusion. To proceed as if there is anything you can do or avoid doing to control another's thoughts, choices, or behavior is unrealistic and delusional. It is also often fueled by all or nothing thinking that does not see things as they truly are. When something is bad, you may think everything is bad. When something is good, you may think everything is good. The reality is that even in the worst of times, there are still some good things and even in the best of times, everything is not perfect.

The sexual brokenness of a loved one has already cost you dearly. Don't compound your losses by attempting to control people or circumstances over which you have no control. There is a cost for control.

Day Four Assignments

1. Peace is possible regardless of what is going on around you. *"Whoever dwells in the shelter of the Most High will rest in the shadow of the Almighty. I will say of the Lord, 'He is my refuge and my fortress, my God, in whom I trust'"* (Psalm 91:1-2). If you are relying on your ability to control things to bring you peace, you will be disappointed. If you trust in the Lord for your future, you will have peace. Are you lacking peace right now? Could it be a result of your own attempts to control things instead of trusting in God? If that's you, explain. __

   _____

   _____

   _____

2. Have you missed opportunities to experience the joy of the moment because you were focused on how to control someone or something hoping to avoid pain in the future? If so, explain. _____

   _____

   _____

   _____

3. Do you find yourself exhausted from trying to manage the lives of others? Do you believe letting go of that control can actually bring freedom? Yes ☐ No ☐

4. Do you feel filled with anxiety? If so, has it negatively impacted you physically or mentally in any way? If so, explain. _____

   _____

   _____

   _____

5. Do you experience periods of extreme, all or nothing thinking? Yes ☐ No ☐ Could this be causing you to grasp for control? Yes ☐ No ☐

Next Step: Ask God to give you a realistic picture of what your efforts to control have cost you and how freedom from that might look.

Day Five
Victory through Surrender

In November of 2018, the driver of a train in Australia stepped off the train to investigate what he thought was a problem. While on the ground, the train departed without him. The runaway train, at the average speed of 68 mph, careened out of control for almost an hour. Eventually the train was deliberately derailed, creating a dramatic scene of crumpled and twisted metal.

If you are the victim of sexual betrayal, perhaps you can relate to that train driver. You may feel like your life is on a runaway collision course and you have no power to stop it. That feeling of having no control naturally strikes great fear within.

Often when a person realizes she has no control over her circumstances, she feels vulnerable to attack. She imagines being hurt and begins to feel psychologically created pain. This may drive her to do everything possible to prevent further injury, including desperately trying to control the people and circumstances in her life. If your trauma has led you to this, you've likely experienced the vicious cycle of fear, control, and helplessness. How do you stop this crazy train?

1. Get real.

In Genesis, God promised Abraham a son even though he and his wife Sarah were very old. Years went by and Sarah still hadn't conceived a child. Frustrated to have not seen progress, Sarah decided to "help" God by giving her maid to her husband to produce an heir. This resulted in a son but also brought great problems because it wasn't God's way or his timing.

It is important to be honest with yourself. Have you been frustrated because you haven't seen changes in your spouse or circumstances as quickly as you'd like? How have you taken matters into your own hands? Admit how you may have attempted to control the people in your life by controlling their circumstances in an effort to prevent further pain. It's the first step toward freedom.

2. Get support.

Find a trustworthy friend whom you can tell of your struggle with controlling behaviors and of your desire to change. This should be someone you know will pray for you and hold you accountable.

3. Make a benefits list.

We've seen the cost of controlling. What would the benefits be of releasing those attempts to control? Consider the difference it would make in your life. Certainly it would produce more peace and joy. Imagine the freedom from trying to run others' lives. Consider the benefits to your physical and mental well-being.

4. Embrace trust.

Our attempts to control people, circumstances and our future demonstrate a lack of faith in God. We, in effect, are attempting to play God: a role we are ill-equipped to perform. *"Cease striving and know that I am God"* (Psalm 46:10 NASB). When we acknowledge that we are not God and that there is One infinitely wiser and more powerful, taking the leap of faith to trust him becomes a little easier.

5. Surrender.

I was familiar with the Serenity Prayer, but when I began recovery, it became a part of my everyday life and it was a game changer. The desire to control is a daily battle and there must be a daily battle plan. Reciting it reminds me that there is much in my life I cannot control. But I can hand it all over to an all-powerful, all-knowing and all-loving God.

> *God, grant me the serenity to accept the things I cannot change;*
> *Courage to change the things I can;*
> *And the wisdom to know the difference.*

Day Five Assignments

Many years ago, we got a kitten. She was adorable and curious. One day, I heard her crying out in pain. She was under the recliner in which I was sitting. This was a nice plush one with a massager and heat controls so it had cords underneath. Taby had gotten one of the cords wrapped around her paw. The more she pulled to free herself, the tighter it became. As I attempted to help her, in her pain, she scratched and bit me. She did not have the wisdom or the vantage point to see that all of her efforts were only making it worse. She did not have the means to free herself. I had the knowledge and the power to do so, but she wouldn't let me. There were brief moments, when in her exhaustion, she struggled less and I would rush in to help. But once again, she began pulling and fighting against me. Finally, I made the decision to get scissors and cut the cord, ruining the controls but freeing the kitten.

How often are we like that little kitten? We find ourselves in a situation that is causing us great pain and we do everything in our limited power to eliminate the pain. God is standing by to help and guide us, but in our pain, we fight for control and we make matters worse. To experience freedom and peace, we must learn to surrender control to the only One who has the vantage point, wisdom, and power to direct our lives.

1. Make a list of the primary people in your life and honestly admit how you have tried to control them by anger, shame, criticism, withholding love, sex, praise, or affection. Consider how you may have tried to control them by controlling their circumstances. "Go home and let all your relatives off the potter's wheel. You are not the potter!" - Joyce Meyer

   _____
   _____
   _____
   _____
   _____
   _____
   _____

2. Write the name of someone with whom you can share your desire and efforts to surrender attempts to control others. Ask that person to pray for you and hold you accountable.

   _____

3. Make a list of benefits you will receive by letting go of your attempts to control others.

   _____
   _____
   _____
   _____

4. Embrace trust. There is a slogan in 12-step recovery that says, "Act as if." You may not completely trust God yet, but how would your life look if you did? How would you allow him to control the people in your life and your circumstances if you did trust him?

   _____
   _____
   _____
   _____

5. As an act of surrender, pray the Serenity Prayer daily and every time you are tempted to control others or circumstances that aren't yours to control.

   God, grant me the serenity to accept the things I cannot change;
   Courage to change the things I can;
   And the wisdom to know the difference.

Next Step: Confess to God your attempts to control people and things other than yourself. Ask him to give you a willing heart and the faith to relinquish that control to him.

WEEK FIVE
Anger

"If you spend your time hoping someone will suffer the consequences for what they did to your heart, then you're allowing them to hurt you a second time in your mind."

- Shannon L. Alder

Day One
Crossing the Line

Introduction: Is anger wrong?

Anger is a God-given emotion. There are several occasions in Scripture that tell of Jesus becoming angry at sin and injustice. Certainly, sexual sins anger God and understandably anger those betrayed by them. While anger alone is not a sin, the Bible contains many warnings concerning it. Ephesians 4:26 says, *"In your anger do not sin."* When does it cross the line into sin?

"Do not let any unwholesome talk come out of your mouths, but only what is helpful for building others up according to their needs, that it may benefit those who listen" (Ephesians 4:29). We cross the line into sin when we say things that are hurtful, degrading, or in any way attack a person's worth and tear him or her down.

Purpose of Anger

We were given what psychologists call a fight or flight nature. When we experience something threatening, it can lead to an anger that puts us in the fight mode and serves to protect us. That fight may not be physical. If we see an evil or injustice, the resulting anger can motivate us to fight to protect those being harmed or to fight for change. There are times when threatened, we switch to flight mode and attempt to flee from the perceived threat.

In our society today, we seldom experience threats to our physical well-being, yet we often respond to threats to our emotional well-being with anger. This anger serves a number of purposes including:

1. To mask emotions such as fear, hurt, or sadness

Often we think these masked emotions make us appear weak and vulnerable. To cover that, we utilize anger to empower and protect ourselves. The puffer fish is a relatively slow fish that when threatened will inflate its body to appear larger and to make itself more difficult to be eaten. Similarly, we sometimes use anger as a defense to make us appear a more formidable foe.

2. To get attention

If we don't feel validated or heard, we may use anger to get the attention we feel is lacking.

3. To self-soothe

Steven Stosny, in his book *Treating Attachment Abuse*, explains that when angry, the brain secretes the hormone, norepinephrine, which is experienced by the organism as an analgesic. Individuals confronted with physical or psychological pain, or the threat of pain, can internally activate the anger response that will release the chemical that will numb the pain.

4. To feel in control

We utilize anger in an attempt to change or alter someone's behavior when what we really want is to change their heart. This method has little chance of producing lasting behavioral change and has no chance of changing the heart. Shannon Alder says, "Anger, resentment and jealousy don't change the heart of others; it only changes yours."

5. To identify an unmet need

Dr. Marshall Rosenberg, founder of Nonviolent Communication Process, says, "At the core of all anger is a need that is not being fulfilled."

Day One Assignments

Imagine going into a library with no database and attempting to find a particular book on the shelves among thousands of books without knowing where to begin. Identifying our feelings can be much the same for most of us. It is a skill that can be learned, but few individuals are taught how to identify, process, or communicate emotions while growing up. Often our tendency is to stuff emotions and distract ourselves with busyness.

A key component to any recovery is learning how to recognize emotion, explore its cause, and process it in a healthy way. As was said under the purpose of anger, anger often is a mask for other emotions. To address anger or any other emotion, we must first be able to identify it. The following exercise is intended to help you begin to put a label on what you are feeling and explore your earliest memory of that same feeling. Begin this exercise now and continue doing it once a day for several weeks as you consider a different feeling each time, alternating between positive and negative ones.

Feeling Exercise

1. I feel (<u>feeling word</u>) when _____. (present tense)

2. I first remember feeling (<u>same feeling word</u>) when _____. (past tense)

Example:
I feel peaceful when I am at the beach listening to the waves and seeing the beautiful water.
I first remember feeling peaceful when I was a little girl and would sit in my daddy's lap.

Next Step: Ask God to give you wisdom and an understanding heart so you can rightly discern your emotions.

Day Two
All the Rage

The medical community, psychologists, and the Bible all agree that anger can be dangerous and harmful. While anger as a result of your spouse's sexual acting out is understandable, it is not without risk if allowed to fester or if not dealt with properly. As an added word of caution, be careful with whom you share your story. You will likely have family members and close friends who will sympathize with you and will be all too happy to throw lighter fluid on the fire of your anger. Carefully choose safe individuals who ultimately have your healing at heart.

Anger can have a negative impact on you spiritually, emotionally, relationally, and physically. Mark Twain said, "Anger is an acid that can do more harm to the vessel in which it is stored than to anything on which it is poured." What are some of the harmful effects of anger?

1. Anger can eliminate your peace.

Anger and peace cannot coexist. Either anger will drive out peace or peace will drive out anger.

2. Anger can cause a wedge between you and God.

Anger can cause us to blame God for our circumstances or can at least hamper our desire to talk to him. If we've crossed the line and allowed our anger to lead us to sin by tearing another person down with our words or actions, that breaks our fellowship with God. It will remain broken until we admit that to God and the other party and change our ways.

3. Anger clouds our perception.

Anger causes us to magnify another's faults while minimizing our own. *"Why do you see the speck that is in your brother's eye and do not notice the log in your own eye?"* (Matthew 7:3 ESV).

4. Anger can lead us to act foolishly.

Ambrose Bierce said, "Speak when you are angry and you will make the best speech you will ever regret." Solomon said, *"A quick-tempered man acts foolishly"* (Proverbs 14:17 NASB).

5. Anger can damage relationships.

"A hot-tempered person stirs up conflict" (Proverbs 15:18). We can say and do things when we are angry that we would never say or do otherwise. If you throw a dart at a dartboard, you can remove the dart but the hole remains. We can later apologize but we can't undo the damage.

6. Anger can cause many health issues.

"When I refused to confess my sin, my body wasted away, and I groaned all day long" (Psalm 32:3 NLT). Medical studies have shown that continual or repeated anger can weaken the immune system, cause high blood pressure, depression, sleep disorders, gastrointestinal problems, heightened anxiety, and can greatly increase the risk of heart attack or stroke.

Day Two Assignments

1. Continue doing your daily Feeling Exercise.

2. Begin keeping an anger journal this week. Write down every instance when you feel angry.

3. Are you currently battling feelings of anger? Yes □ No □

4. In the past, have you acted foolishly in your anger? Explain. _____
    _____
    _____
    _____

5. Are you experiencing any health issues currently that might be the result of anger? Yes □ No □ If so, describe them. _____
    _____
    _____

6. Do you feel at a loss to control your anger? Yes □ No □

7. Are you currently angry at God? Yes □ No □

Action Step: Ask God to help you recognize when you are feeling angry and to help you begin processing that anger in a healthy way.

Day Three
Toxic Waste

In the 1980s, I lived in Friendswood, Texas, just five miles from the beautiful, new subdivision of South Bend. Developers bought the property from a bankrupt refinery. Residents of that community began experiencing numerous health issues and women reported a higher than average number of miscarriages and babies born with birth defects.

The problem was that the refinery had buried toxic waste in large pits all over the property and it seeped through the soil into the pipes of the new subdivision. People abandoned their homes, and eventually the area was deserted, and all that remains are large fences and signs warning people to stay away.

Unhealthy anger becomes like that toxic waste. It seeps into all areas of your life and can cause irreparable damage to your health and relationships. Unhealthy types of angry people harbor unhealthy types of anger. Let's take a look at each.

1. **Unhealthy Types of Anger**

   a. Sarcasm ("At least you were kind enough to wait until I was asleep to watch porn!")
   b. Passive Aggressive ("Accidentally" burn his dinner.)
   c. Verbal Abuse ("You're such a loser!")
   d. Blaming ("I wouldn't have lost my job if you hadn't wrecked our lives!")
   e. Retaliatory (Have an affair, go on a shopping spree.)
   f. Rage (Smash his computer.)
   g. Isolation (Withdraw.)
   h. Depression (Anger is turned inward.)

2. **Unhealthy Types of Angry People**

   a. Compliant Stuffer – try to keep peace
   b. Controlling Spewer – attack and demand

We want to take steps to make sure we do not allow our anger to turn toxic and that we are people who process anger in a healthy way. Over the next two days, we will consider healthy anger and anger management.

Day Three Assignments

"Holding on to anger is like grasping a hot coal with the intent of throwing it at someone else; you are the one who gets burned." (Buddha)

1. Do you tend to be the compliant stuffer who tries to keep the peace or the controlling spewer, prone to attack and demand? _____
_____

2. Consider the unhealthy types of anger mentioned in today's lesson. Rank them in the order in which you are most likely to use them with 1 being the most likely and 8 being the least likely.

____ Sarcasm ("At least you were kind enough to wait until I was asleep to watch porn!")
____ Passive Aggressive ("Accidentally" burn his dinner.)
____ Verbal Abuse ("You're such a loser!")
____ Blaming ("I wouldn't have lost my job if you hadn't wrecked our lives!")
____ Retaliatory (Have an affair, go on a shopping spree.)
____ Rage (Smash his computer.)
____ Isolation (Withdraw.)
____ Depression (Anger is turned inward.)

3. Continue your daily feeling exercise and your anger journal.

"Search me, God, and know my heart; test me and know my anxious thoughts. See if there is any offensive way in me, and lead me in the way everlasting" (Psalm 139:23-24).

Next Step: Pray Psalm 139:23-24 to God, asking him to reveal any ways you have shown unhealthy anger. Ask him to forgive you and to take that from you.

Day Four
Healthy Anger

"But the wisdom that is from above is first pure, then peaceable, gentle, and easy to be intreated, full of mercy and good fruits, without partiality, and without hypocrisy" (James 3:17 KJV).

I believe this verse not only describes wisdom, but also lists attributes of a healthy, God-like anger. Here are some more characteristics of healthy anger.

1. Controlled

"Fools vent their anger, but the wise quietly hold it back" (Proverbs 29:11 NLT). Healthy anger is responsive rather than reactive. It is measured, considered, and released appropriately.

2. Honest

"We will speak the truth in love, growing in every way more and more like Christ" (Ephesians 4:15 NLT). Healthy anger does not exaggerate or embellish. It is not convinced that feelings and thoughts are necessarily true, but investigates and evaluates to ascertain facts.

3. Fair

"Do to others as you would like them to do to you" (Luke 6:31). Healthy anger is compassionate. Instead of judging others by their actions and ourselves by our intent, we judge both with the same measure.

4. Responsible

Healthy anger takes responsibility for one's own feelings and actions rather than blaming with statements such as "You made me..." It is expressed with "I" statements.

5. Constructive

Adam Grant cites research which indicates that when we're angry *at* others, we aim for retaliation or revenge. But when we're angry *for* others, we seek out justice and a better system. We don't just want to punish; we want to help.

6. Current

"Do not call to mind the former things, or ponder things of the past" (Isaiah 43:18 NASB). Healthy anger does not dredge up things from the past but focuses on the current issue.

7. Communicative

Healthy anger does not wait to be guessed, figured out, or uncovered. Nor does it veil itself in sarcasm or covert retaliation. Rather it is expressed clearly.

8. Realistic

Healthy anger does not blame others for things beyond their control but is realistic in its scope and proportion.

Day Four Assignments

Wow! Keeping anger in healthy bounds is not easy. In fact, I'd say that apart from reliance on the power of God, we don't stand a chance. The wounds caused by sexual betrayal run so deep and hurt so badly, they seem to take over and manifest with such toxicity that if we aren't deliberate in our efforts to keep them under control, they will cause destruction. If we are honest, there are times we just don't care. We feel justified in lashing out in whatever manner we like. But as we saw earlier this week, the harmful results will likely further complicate our lives.

1. Take some time to really consider the thing in your life that currently has you the angriest. Write an anger letter expressing that as colorfully as you'd like. Forget the healthy guidelines for a few minutes and just express what you are really feeling. (This is not to be shared with anyone.)

2. Now reconsider the matter and evaluate it in light of today's guidelines. Is what you're angry about based 100 percent in truth or have you exaggerated it in your mind in any way? Are you responding fairly? Is this a current issue or have you reached back into the past? Is your goal to be restorative and constructive, or is it to be punitive? Can you communicate about this issue clearly? Do you feel your level of anger is in proportion to the offense?

3. Continue your daily feeling exercise and your anger journal.

Next Step: Ask God if the issue you listed in the above assignment is something you need to communicate to the offending party at this time. If so, ask God to give you the wisdom and control to communicate it in a healthy way.

Day Five
Anger Management

It would take a rare, and I'd dare say emotionally detached woman to experience a husband's sexual betrayal and not have some level of anger. If you are reading this material, that probably is not you. So how do we manage the anger that comes as a result of this trauma?

1. Practice good self-care.

When we are tired, hungry, sleep deprived, or have some other unaddressed need, we are more prone to extreme reaction. Make sure healthy eating, adequate sleep, exercise, and relaxation are a part of your routine care.

2. Identify the cause.

Take the time to really assess what you're feeling and try to establish the root cause. Often, the surface issue is not the real issue. For example, if your husband is late coming home from work and you find yourself feeling overwhelmed with anger, it is probably not because his boss called him into the office at the last minute and you had to delay dinner. It is more likely coming from a fear that he wasn't at the office but had met a sexual partner on the way home.

3. Take deep breaths.

Anger causes our heart rate and blood pressure to increase. The fight or flight mode kicks in and blood rushes to our limbs to ready us for action. Our brain is operating on survival mode and not on the reasoning and logic level. Taking deep breaths can slow your heart rate and lower your blood pressure.

4. Take a time-out.

Before you react, step back and take a time-out. Remove yourself from the person or the setting if necessary, to regroup and consider how to respond rather than react.

5. Avoid extreme thinking.

It can be easy to slip into exaggerated, all or nothing thinking. Avoid thoughts that include the words *always* or *never*. Try to avoid reading things into a situation that are not there. Example: You asked your husband to bring home a loaf of bread and he forgot. You start thinking, "He doesn't love and respect me. He never does anything I ask. I can't count on him for anything." There is a slight chance that is true. But more likely he's absent minded and just forgot!

6. Pray.

Ask God to help you to consider the matter calmly, clearly, and truthfully.

7. Do an anger exercise.

Write an anger letter. (Don't share it.) Read the letter out loud when you're alone. Get a plastic bat or racket and hit a pillow repeatedly while yelling, until you are tired. (Do that when you are home alone.)

8. Calmly share your feelings with a trusted friend, sponsor, or counselor.

9. Consider possible solutions.

Day Five Assignments

1. Continue your daily feeling exercise and anger journal.

2. Look at each instance recorded in your anger journal and consider:

   a. Had I been practicing good self-care prior to the incident?

   b. What thoughts were going through my mind?

   c. Did I respond in a healthy manner?

   d. Is there an unmet need in my life that requires attention?

   e. How could I have responded better?

Next Step: Take the time to regularly read the anger management tips and ask God to help those become a part of your life and the way you respond to anger.

WEEK SIX
Boundaries

*"Boundaries represent awareness, knowing what the
limits are and then respecting those limits."*

\- David W. Earle

Day One
The Whats and Whys of Boundaries

Sandy has a neighbor who shows up at her house every evening when she gets home from work and dominates her time, making it difficult for her to accomplish anything or to just sit and relax. Sandy feels stuck, frustrated and resentful, but she doesn't want to hurt her neighbor's feelings.

Lucy has a boss who loses his temper easily and raises his voice. She feels like she has to walk on eggshells around him. She feels anxious at work and hates the environment but says she can't quit because she needs the job.

What do these two scenarios have in common? In both instances, these women have failed to set healthy boundaries and have taken on the victim role. We wear that label when we act as if we have no choice or say in a matter. The reality is there are rarely situations when we have no choice. We may not like or be comfortable with those choices, but they are available.

Setting boundaries is a skill that is learned over time. If it wasn't learned while growing up, it can be more difficult to learn and implement in adulthood. It is important for each person to know they have a right to protect and defend themselves. There can be a lot of confusion about boundaries, what they are, what they aren't, and why they are important. In the space below, I will begin to answer those questions.

What they are. Boundaries are . . .

- Personal limits
- Markers where one person ends and the other begins
- External expressions of internal limits

What they aren't. Healthy boundaries are not . . .

- A means to control
- An attempt to manipulate
- A threat

Why they are needed. Boundaries . . .

- Are a part of good self-care
- Help guard against resentments
- Help us take responsibility for our own feelings
- Demonstrate self-respect

You get what you tolerate.

Day One Assignments

Part of setting healthy boundaries requires speaking up for what we need. This can feel uncomfortable if we're not accustomed to doing so. This can be further complicated if we are learning this skill while experiencing the trauma caused by the sexual betrayal of a spouse. In this situation, the natural tendency is to use boundaries in an attempt to affect the behavior of the addict. While we may know we can't control them, subconsciously we may design boundaries with that goal. How can we know the difference? Let's look at a few examples.

Part 1: Boundaries as a means to . . .

1. Control – "You can't go out with your friends."
2. Manipulate – You purposely schedule other things to keep him from going out with friends.
3. Threat – "If you go out with your friends, I'm taking the kids and leaving!"
4. Punishment – "You can't initiate sex for at least a week since you went out with your friends."

Consider the examples above and list at least two ways you have used boundaries in an attempt to change someone's behavior.

1. _____

2. _____

Part 2: Boundaries as a need for . . .

1. Self-care – When we fail to set boundaries, we often find ourselves feeling exhausted and overwhelmed because we are doing things for others they should be doing for themselves.
2. Avoiding resentments – We can become resentful when we expect others to read our minds and know what we need, and they don't possess that superpower.

3. Taking responsibility for our own feelings – When we make statements such as, "You make me angry" or "You make me feel unwanted," we are giving someone else the power over our emotions instead of taking the responsibility for them ourselves.

4. Demonstrating self-respect – When we allow others to run all over us and we don't step in to stop it, we demonstrate a disregard for our right to be treated with respect and to be protected.

Consider the examples in Part 2, and list at least two ways you have set or failed to set healthy boundaries similarly.

1. _____

2. _____

Next Step: Ask God to give you an understanding about healthy boundaries, their need, and how to implement them into your life.

Day Two
Why We Fail to Set Boundaries

"Daring to set boundaries is about having the courage to love ourselves, even when we risk disappointing others." (Brené Brown)

If boundaries are a crucial part of self-care, why are so many people hesitant to set them in their lives? I believe one of the greatest obstacles to setting boundaries is the false belief that it is somehow rude or selfish to set boundaries. Those who consider themselves followers of God particularly seem to struggle with this misguided idea. Feelings of guilt often arise at even the thought of considering our own needs.

So are boundaries in opposition to God's will for our lives? When Jesus was asked which was the greatest commandment, he said, *"You must love the Lord your God with all your heart, all your soul, and all your mind"* (Matthew 22:37 NLT). Though not asked, he went on to state another commandment which he said was equally important. *"Love your neighbor as yourself"* (Matthew 22:39 NLT). We are quick to focus on the part about loving our neighbor but gloss over how we are to love them. We are to love them as we love ourselves. We must love and respect ourselves enough to set healthy boundaries. Part of loving our neighbors is respecting their boundaries.

Beyond this foundational obstacle to setting boundaries, what are some other reasons we may fail to set boundaries?

1. Lack of knowledge

As we saw yesterday, setting boundaries is a learned skill. We must first recognize we have a need for them and then we must learn the proper way to implement them.

2. Discomfort

Anything new can push us out of our comfort zone and initially cause stress. It is important to focus on the long term benefit instead of the temporary discomfort.

3. Perceived as controlling

At first, we may feel like we are being controlling by setting boundaries. As we begin setting boundaries, those who are not accustomed to that may accuse us of being controlling. That's not usually a welcomed label.

4. Met with resistance

As was just pointed out in number three, those in our lives who aren't used to us having boundaries may not respond positively when we begin setting them. The new boundaries may be met by anger, tears, or resentment. And there will likely be those who ignore or violate them, at least in the beginning.

5. Must surrender the outcome

When a boundary is set in a healthy way, the focus is on ourselves and what we need. We let go of the attempt to use that boundary to control another and we surrender their responses and the outcome.

6. Fear of the loss of love

If we have fear of abandonment or fear of being alone, we may think that sacrificing what we need is the way to avoid that. But then our relationship is based on lies. Other people can't truly know and love us if we fail to communicate our needs and what is important to us.

Day Two Assignments

There is a debate in our country over the construction of borders. Many are saying that erecting any barrier that keeps people out is unkind; some even say it's evil. Ironically, some of those same people live in homes surrounded by large fences to keep others out and their homes are equipped with locking doors and a security system. How is that different? In the case of national borders, people may not see a direct impact from a lack of them, as opposed to their own homes, where a lack of fences, door locks and alarm systems is more likely to have a direct adverse effect on them.

My purpose in referencing this issue is not to support or disparage either side in the matter. It is simply to make the point that as with the border issue, there are those who will accuse individuals with boundaries of being selfish or unkind while they themselves have boundaries in their own lives for their own physical, mental, and emotional well-being. This is the kind of criticism that contributes to the reluctance of some to establish boundaries in their personal lives.

1. Do you have strong and consistent boundaries in your life?
Yes ☐ No ☐

2. If you are lacking boundaries, what is holding you back from establishing them? _____
_____
_____
_____

3. Do you feel adequately equipped with the knowledge to set boundaries?
Yes ☐ No ☐

4. In the past, have you had boundaries that were met with resistance?
Yes ☐ No ☐

5. Does the fear of disappointing others make you hesitant to set boundaries? Yes ☐ No ☐

6. Name one thing that you think you need in order to be better able to set healthy boundaries in your life. _____
_____

Next Step: Ask God to remove any mental obstacle in your thinking that is hindering you from setting healthy boundaries in your life.

Day Three
Know the Need

The Bible tells the story of a man named Nehemiah who was a Jewish exile living in Persia when he received word from his people about the condition of his homeland. They told him that the wall of Jerusalem was broken down and that the gates had been burned with fire. Though groups of the Jewish exiles had been permitted to return home, Nehemiah knew that for them to have protection from surrounding enemies so they could grow into a healthy nation again, a strong wall was crucial.

"When I heard these things, I sat down and wept. For some days I mourned and fasted and prayed before the God of heaven" (Nehemiah 1:4). After grieving over the situation, the first thing Nehemiah did was seek God's direction. The story goes on to say that he went to the king and asked for permission to return to the city of Judah to rebuild the wall. Once he was back in Jerusalem, he spent several days assessing the need before he began the project of rebuilding the wall.

For you to grow into the strong and healthy individual God has created you to be, you must have boundaries in your life. If those have been previously inconsistent, unhealthy, or completely lacking, there are things that need to be in place before you can implement them. Like Nehemiah, you need to ask for God's direction and assess the situation before attempting to construct new boundaries.

What is needed to construct and live with healthy boundaries?

1. The ability to attach to others without giving up a sense of self

Children learn healthy attachment when they are provided a safe environment where their needs are met and they are encouraged to explore their own likes and creativity. This is fundamental in healthy relationships. When that experience is lacking, it can be difficult for adults to attach to others in a healthy way. They can be completely self-centered and needy or on the other end, they can attach to another but completely lose all sense of self. In marriage, one of the partners can become so absorbed with the spouse that he or she forsakes individual interests, values, and ideas for the coupleship. This is not uncommon when addiction is present because the spouse can become consumed with the demands and needs of the addict to the neglect of her own needs. Regardless of the cause, if an individual is lacking the ability to attach to others without giving up a sense of self, some work or therapy in that area will be necessary before there will be consistent success in setting healthy boundaries.

2. The ability to say "no" without fearing loss

According to Ori and Ram Brafman, authors of *Sway: The Irresistible Pull of Irrational Behavior*, we often make poor decisions simply to avoid loss. But the reality is that almost every decision involves the loss of something. You choose one thing over another. Avoiding saying no doesn't prevent loss. It may just determine the loss. If I say yes to something I don't want to do out of fear that I might lose the approval or relationship of another, I lose the opportunity to do what I'd prefer to do and I lose inner peace. Author and personal coach, Cheryl Richardson says, "If you avoid conflict to keep the peace, you start a war inside yourself." Before you can set and keep healthy boundaries, you have to let go of the fear of loss that may result from saying no.

3. The ability to take "no" from others without withdrawing emotionally

We will never be comfortable setting boundaries for ourselves if we aren't comfortable with the right for others to have them. We need to respect the boundaries of others without seeing them as a personal affront. If I ask someone to spend the evening with me and they decline, I don't have to shut down emotionally. It may or may not have anything to do with me. Either way, it is that person's right to make that decision and I need to respect the boundary.

4. The ability to discern where boundaries are needed

As we saw in the story of Nehemiah, it is important to assess where the work is needed. In regard to boundaries, feelings are often a clue to their deficit. When I begin feeling overwhelmed, stressed, or resentful, it is likely that there are boundaries I can put in place that will help prevent that in the future. The feelings exercise can be beneficial in helping us to recognize those emotions.

Day Three Assignments

Recognizing the signs of unhealthy boundaries is vital to establishing healthy ones. Read the following list of unhealthy boundaries and put a check by any that you see in your life.

___ Going against personal values or rights to please others

___ Letting others define you

___ Not speaking up when treated poorly

___ Believing others can anticipate your needs

___ Falling apart when someone can't take care of you

___ Feeling bad or guilty about saying "no"

___ Allowing others to describe your reality

___ Feelings of resentment

___ Accepting food, gifts, advances, touches, or sex that you don't want

___ Letting others direct your life

___ Indiscriminately sharing details of your life to others

___ Allowing others to take all they can from you

Next Step: Ask God to help you discern signs of unhealthy boundaries in your life and where you need to set healthy boundaries.

Day Four
How to Establish Healthy Boundaries

If you did not see it before, the lessons this week may have awakened your realization that you need healthy boundaries in your life. But if you are like many people, you may have no idea how to go about incorporating them into your life. Consider the following steps for establishing healthy boundaries.

1. Recognize your limits.

Feelings of stress, anxiousness, and discomfort can be signs that you have reached your limit. Learn your physical, emotional and mental capacities.
Example: "I feel overwhelmed every time my daughter asks me to babysit her children."

2. Determine what you need.

Example: "I need to feel like my health isn't at risk when I have sexual relations with my partner."

3. Identify the boundary.

What boundary do you need to put in place to honor your limits and meet your need?
Example: "I will not go out more than one night each week."

4. Communicate without blaming.

It is important to own your boundary and keep the focus on yourself.
Example: "When you do (action), I feel (emotion)."

5. Identify the consequence.

A boundary without a consequence is an empty threat. For a boundary to be effective, there needs to be a consequence.
Example: "If you raise your voice at me, I will leave the room."

6. Don't apologize.

You have a right to determine your needs and to take responsibility for seeing they are met by setting healthy boundaries. Author Anne Lamott says, "'No' is a complete sentence."

7. Get support and accountability.

If can be difficult to set boundaries when you aren't accustomed to doing so. Having a sponsor, counselor, or trusted friend to talk with and who will hold you accountable is a valuable asset.

Day Four Assignments

1. Identify a current situation in your life that is causing you to feel uncomfortable, stressed, or anxious.
Example: "My husband yells at me when he is frustrated."

_____

_____

2. Name one thing that you think would reduce the tension you feel in the situation listed in number one.
Example: "I would feel less anxious if my husband would speak to me in a normal tone when he is frustrated."

_____

_____

3. How can you address the situation with a healthy boundary?
Example: "I will not tolerate my husband yelling at me."

_____

_____

4. Write out how you might communicate your need and boundary without blaming.
Incorrect way: "When you get frustrated and yell at me, you make me feel afraid. You can't yell at me anymore."
Correct way: "When you are frustrated and raise your voice to me, I feel afraid. I want you to speak to me only when you can do so in a calm voice."

_____

_____

_____

5. Determine a consequence for the boundary violation.
Example: "If you speak to me with a raised voice, I will remind you one time. If you continue, I will take the kids and go for a drive."

_____

_____

_____

6. Name one safe person with whom you can share your attempt to create healthy boundaries.

Example: A trusted friend, sponsor, or counselor

_____

Next Step: Ask God to equip you to set and communicate healthy boundaries. Ask someone to hold you accountable.

Day Five
Dealing with Resistance

The path of least resistance and least trouble is a mental rut already made. It requires troublesome work to undertake the altering of old beliefs. (John Dewey)

We are creatures of habit and usually resistant to change. This is often evident when dealing with new boundaries. If we are the ones constructing new boundaries and we aren't accustomed to doing so, it will take time and practice for it to become a new healthy habit. Expect resistance but don't let it deter you. Having some idea of what it may look like and how to deal with it will likely bring some sense of comfort as you move forward.

1. Internal Resistance – the pressure within ourselves to settle for the status quo rather than putting forth the effort needed for change.

    a. Reward – The decision to draw a boundary is usually the result of some discomfort with our current situation. But when we experience difficulty attempting to establish a new habit, it is tempting to get frustrated and cease trying. It is important to focus on the end goal and push past the internal stress that usually accompanies the work of any new habit.

    b. Rewire – Our failure to set healthy boundaries in the past is at least partially due to our own internal chatter. Things such as "My needs don't matter," "I'm being selfish," or "I might be rejected" will need to be replaced with self-talk that helps push you past your own resistance. There needs to be a new loop that includes phrases such as "I am worthy of love and respect" and "I am responsible for my own feelings and well-being."

    c. Repercussion – Setting a consequence for crossing your personal boundaries, or for failing to maintain or enforce your boundaries, can be a motivator for change. If I've established that I need three nights a week by myself to go to the gym so I can burn off stress and take care of my body but then I don't do it; if I have

116

set a consequence of washing the windows, when I hate washing windows, this serves as a motivator to respect the importance of the boundary.

2. External Resistance – the opposition from others that may manifest as anger, pouting, withdrawal, threats, guilt messages, or disregard.

   a. Acknowledge – It is important to acknowledge the resistant party's feelings. You might try saying something like, "I can see that you are angry, but I cannot...(your boundary)."
   b. Recognize – If someone responds negatively, recognize that it is his or her issue, not yours.
   c. Clarify – Perhaps there is honest confusion regarding your boundary. George Bernard Shaw said, "The single biggest problem in communication is the illusion that it has taken place."
   d. Composure – Stay calm. Don't attack or respond with anger or raised voice.
   e. Don't debate – Simply restate your boundary and possibly the need behind it but don't engage in argument.
   f. Maintain – Resist the pressure or temptation to discard your boundary as a result of the other person's negative response. A toddler will throw a fit to get his way. The parent who gives in will become a pawn in the child's life. Likewise, altering your stance based on someone's resistance will only reinforce selfishness. *"A hot-tempered person must pay the penalty; rescue them and, you will have to do it again"* (Proverbs 19:19).
   g. Respect – Just as you want others to respect your decision to erect a boundary, you must respect their choice to not comply. You may not like it, but you can't control them.
   h. Release – Be prepared to enact your consequence for a broken boundary, or if it is an untenable situation, to walk away.

Day Five Assignments

Healthy boundaries yield great rewards. They offer us stability and give us more control over our lives. They can help us learn to better communicate with others and can lead to more fulfilling relationships. Unfortunately, there is no quick and easy way to establish them. It takes time, hard work, and persistence. *"Let perseverance finish its work so that you may be mature and complete, not lacking anything"* (James 1:4).

Since the rewards for consistent healthy boundaries may not be immediately seen, we need motivation to keep us pressing on. Dr. Henry Cloud says, "We change our behavior when the pain of staying the same becomes greater than the pain of changing. Consequences give us the pain that motivates us to change." Take some time to consider which consequences may motivate you.

Example 1: Sue has a personal boundary to not become physical when she is angry with her husband. Her plan is to leave the room when she is so angry she feels she may become violent. If she fails to do so and becomes physical, she has determined that her consequence will include a written letter of apology to her husband, making his favorite home-cooked meal, and washing his truck.

Example 2: Regina set a boundary with her son that he could not talk disrespectfully to her. She informed him that if he did, she would remind him one time. If he continued, his consequence would be spending the evening in his room with no TV or video games. Regina set a consequence for herself if she did not follow through with her son's consequence for the broken boundary. She will forego the book club she enjoys attending, for one week.

List five personal consequences you think might motivate you to keep your own boundaries or to exact consequences for those who violate your boundaries.

1. _____

2. _____

3. _____

4. _____

5. _____

Next Step: Consequences motivate change. Start giving yourself consequences for failing to keep your own boundaries or neglecting to enforce boundaries for others.

WEEK SEVEN
Boundary Types

*"Your personal boundaries protect the inner
core of your identity and your right to choices."*

- Gerald Manley Hopkins

Day One
Physical Boundaries

Last week we began the work of understanding and creating healthy boundaries. Boundaries are necessary for society to run smoothly and for relationships to thrive. Their purpose is not to keep others away, but to define the healthiest path to engagement. Relationship coach and speaker Mark Groves says, "Walls keep everybody out. Boundaries teach people where the door is."

We need many different types of boundaries with different people. This week we will consider boundaries in a multitude of areas, beginning with physical boundaries. Physical boundaries can involve anything from your personal space to sexual touching. For today's lesson, we will separate the physical into nonsexual and sexual.

Physical Boundary Violations

Nonsexual

- Getting in your face while talking

- Going through your personal things without permission

- Touching you without permission

- Monopolizing your time

- Unsolicited comments about your body

- Borrowing your possessions without permission

Sexual

- Subjecting you to sexual innuendos, talk, or jokes

- Exposing you to pornography

- Exposing you to STDs

- Demanding sex and not respecting your right to say no

- Minimizing or ignoring your feelings about sex

- Demeaning comments about you sexually

Day One Assignments

Complete the Personal Boundaries Assessment Test.

Place '1' next to the following statements that apply to you.

_____ 1. I often feel guilty about not doing enough for my parents or my spouse.

_____ 2. I feel responsible for making other people happy – my spouse, my parents, my children.

_____ 3. I often share personal information with other people when it is none of their business.

_____ 4. I feel uncomfortable making my own decisions in life.

_____ 5. I often go along with the plans of others, even when I want to do something else.

_____ 6. I often feel I must defend the actions of my parents or my spouse to other people.

_____ 7. I do a lot of work for other people, but I hate to ask anyone to do a favor for me.

_____ 8. My parents discouraged me from moving from home.

_____ 9. I wish I didn't have the responsibilities of an adult.

Place '2' next to the statements that apply to you.

_____ 10. When people criticize me, I accept what they say as true and feel bad about myself.

_____ 11. I often think about mistakes I have made and feel bad about myself.

_____ 12. I feel I can't trust God and feel afraid of him.

_____ 13. My parents frequently shared intimate secrets with me.

_____ 14. I was the favorite child of one of my parents.

_____ 15. My parents did not want me to date or to marry.

_____ 16. One of my parents seemed overly interested in my sexuality and my body.

Place '3' next to the statements that apply to you.

_____ 17. One of my parents preferred my company to their spouse.

_____ 18. I was physically, sexually, verbally, or emotionally abused as a child.

_____ 19. I have been in two or more relationships where I have been physically, sexually, or emotionally abused.

Add up your numbers.

0 to 5 = fairly secure emotional and spiritual boundaries

6 to 9 = significant distortions in your boundaries

10 or more = consider counseling

Day Two
Emotional Boundaries

Emotional boundaries are much like invisible fences used for dogs. You can't see them, but you feel uncomfortable when you cross their line. Healthy emotional boundaries help individuals take responsibility for their own feelings, keep them from taking responsibility for another's feelings and guide them as they determine what feelings are appropriate to share and with whom they should share.

Maintaining any boundary can be difficult, but it is especially challenging when dealing with emotional boundaries to not become too emotional. If setting boundaries is a new practice it is easy to fall back into unhealthy patterns when someone is attempting to make you feel a certain way or accusing you of causing them to feel a certain way. It is important to remember "nobody can use something against you that you're not using against you." You are in charge of your own feelings.

Emotional boundary violations include:

- Being told "you shouldn't feel that way"

- Having your feelings ignored

- Being exposed to uncontrolled anger

- Being called names

- Being exposed to constant whining or pouting

- Being forced to stuff your feelings out of fear

- Having affection withheld

- Being told you are responsible for another person's feelings

Day Two Assignments

Constructing boundaries is a skill and as such requires practice. That will be the focus of this week's assignments. First century B.C. Latin writer Publililus Syrus said, "Practice is the best of all instructors."

1. Identify a physical, sexual, or emotional situation in your life that causes you to feel uncomfortable, stressed, or anxious.
Example: When my mother goes through my personal things, I feel disrespected.

_____

_____

2. Name one thing that you think would reduce the tension you are feeling.
Example: I would feel respected if my mother would ask to see something before snooping on her own.

_____

_____

3. Determine a boundary that you think will address the issue.
Example: I will not permit my mother to go through my personal belongings without asking permission.

_____

_____

4. Write out how you might communicate your need and boundary.
Example: "Mom, I realize you may not mean it this way, but when you go through my personal things without asking, I feel disrespected. If there is something you'd like to see, I would appreciate it if you'd ask me first."

_____

_____

_____

5. Determine a consequence for each broken boundary.
Example: If you continue to go through my personal things without asking, I will cease inviting you to my home. (You need to determine

a consequence ahead of time but you don't necessarily need to communicate it in advance. However, if the individual continues to violate your boundary, you will want to state the consequence and then utilize it with a future violation.)

_____

_____

_____

Next Step: Recognition alone of the importance of boundaries will produce no change. Identify areas in your life that are causing you anxiety, stress or resentment, and begin developing corresponding boundaries.

Day Three
Intellectual Boundaries

Each person is entitled to his or her own thoughts and ideas. If someone belittles yours, there is little to be gained from arguing with that individual. Most of the time, someone like that is not interested in learning truth. *"A fool takes no pleasure in understanding, but only in expressing his opinion"* (Proverbs 18:2 ESV).

If someone is criticizing your intelligence, the smartest thing you can do is set a boundary that protects you from that negativity. Albert Einstein said, "The measure of intelligence is the ability to change." If you have neglected drawing healthy boundaries in the past, make a change and begin setting them now.

Intellectual boundary violations include:

- Being told you are stupid

- Having your ability to reason things out discounted

- Being told you will fail

- Having your parenting abilities discounted

- Not being allowed to make everyday choices

- Having your speech or grammar constantly corrected

- Having words put in your mouth

- Being blamed for your children's failures

Day Three Assignments

1. Identify a situation in your life involving an individual belittling or demeaning your intelligence that is causing you to feel uncomfortable, stressed, or anxious.

Example: When I confront my husband about his computer browser history and he tells me I don't know what I'm talking about because I don't know anything about computers, I feel dismissed and ignored.

_____

_____

2. Name one thing that you think would reduce the tension you are feeling.

Example: I would feel heard if my husband would engage in an honest conversation when confronted with suspicious activity on his computer.

_____

_____

3. Determine a boundary that you think will address the issue.

Example: I will not tolerate being belittled and dismissed when I bring a legitimate concern to you regarding your computer activity.

_____

_____

4. Write out how you might communicate your need and boundary.

Example: Sam, I would appreciate it if you would take the time to hear and understand my concerns when I bring up the issue of your computer usage without acting like I know nothing about computers.

_____

_____

_____

5. Determine a consequence for each broken boundary.

Example: If you continue to criticize my level of knowledge about computers instead of honestly addressing my concerns when I bring up an issue about your viewing habits, I will interpret that to mean you are not interested in rebuilding trust and I will spend the next week sleeping in the guest room.

_____

_____

_____

Next Step: The apostle Paul wrote about the importance of thinking on things that are positive (Philippians 4:8). Create boundaries to insulate you from critical and demeaning individuals.

Day Four
Financial Boundaries

People are funny about money. Voltaire said, "When it is a question of money, everybody is of the same religion." One anonymous quote reads, "If you want to be remembered, borrow some money. If you want to be forgotten, lend some." The Bible warns that the love of money is the root of all kinds of evil (I Timothy 6:10). The issue of money has ruined many relationships. Finances are definitely an area in which we are wise to have boundaries in place before issues arise.

Statistics show that 70 percent of lottery winners go broke within five years. Sixty to 70 percent of retiring NFL and NBA players also go broke within five years. Why is that? Large windfalls attract a lot of relatives and friends, all wanting a piece of the pie. The vast majority of lottery winners and professional athletes don't have a financial plan or boundaries around their finances. These things lead to poor financial decisions and mismanagement.

In many marriages, money is used as a means of control. This is another good reason to have financial boundaries in place.

Financial boundary violations include:

- Not being allowed to earn money

- Not being allowed to spend money

- Being pressured to loan money to someone

- Spouse using money designated for household bills on an addiction

- Adult child trying to guilt you into cosigning for a car

- Acquaintance asking how much you paid for your house

- Supervisor divulging your salary to a coworker

- A friend trying to shame you for buying a new dress

Day Four Assignments

1. Identify a financial situation in your life that causes you to feel uncomfortable, stressed, or anxious.
Example: When my husband carries cash, I feel anxious that he may be using it to act out.

_____

_____

2. Name one thing that you think would reduce the tension you are feeling.
Example: I would feel more comfortable if he didn't carry cash.

_____

_____

3. Determine a boundary that you think will address the issue.
Example: My husband carries no more than $10 cash and uses our debit card for spending.

_____

_____

4. Write out how you might communicate your need and boundary.
Example: "Honey, you may have no intention of acting out, but when you carry cash it creates anxiety within me. I'd appreciate it if you would carry no more than $10 cash and instead would use our debit card for spending."

_____

_____

_____

5. Determine a consequence for each broken boundary.

Example: If I see my husband with more than $10 cash, I will remind him one time how important this issue is to me. If he continues, I will let him know that I see that as a sign that he doesn't value my recovery and I will emotionally detach from him.

_____

_____

_____

Next Step: *"No one can serve two masters. Either you will hate the one and love the other, or you will be devoted to the one and despise the other. You cannot serve both God and money"* (Matthew 6:24). Put God first and use his wisdom in setting healthy financial boundaries.

Day Five
Spiritual Boundaries

The two topics most commonly advised to avoid in conversation are politics and religion. People tend to be passionate about their spiritual and religious beliefs or lack thereof. These used to be considered private matters. However, with the creation and popularity of social media, very few things remain private.

This makes for an interesting time in history. We are bombarded with the message about the need for tolerance while at the same time being blasted for individual beliefs. Basically the message is, "You need to be tolerant of my right to believe and live as I want, but if you don't believe like I think you should, I won't tolerate that. I will see that you are publicly shamed and punished." Historically, one of the beautiful things about living in America is the right of every individual to his or her own religious beliefs.

Spiritual boundaries in such an atmosphere can be difficult, but they are necessary. You have the right to your religious, spiritual, and moral beliefs, customs, and values. You have the right to change your beliefs as you wish. No one has the right to pressure you into believing as they do or the right to pressure you into violating your personal morals. You only have to give account to the God of the universe for your spiritual beliefs. It may be helpful to ask yourself, as the apostle Paul asked, *"Am I now seeking the approval of man or of God?"* (Galatians 1:10 ESV).

Spiritual boundary violations may include:

- Being forced into the role of mother or Higher Power to your mate

- Having your relationship with God decided for you

- Having another act as your parent or Higher Power

- Being shamed or mocked for your spiritual beliefs

- Being pressured to violate your own set of morals

- Being told you cannot worship where and how you'd like

- Someone claiming to speak for God and telling you what you should or shouldn't do

Day Five Assignments

"Am I now seeking the approval of man or of God?" (Galatians 1:10 ESV). At the end of it all, we will answer to God alone for our values, morals, and spiritual beliefs and practices. Spiritual boundaries are probably the least prioritized of all, yet should be first on our list.

1. Do you give your spiritual life high priority? Yes ☐ No ☐

2. When someone does something in your presence that goes against your spiritual or moral beliefs, do you say something? Yes ☐ No ☐

3. Have you attempted to play God in a family member's life by judging that person or exacting vengeance? (In Deuteronomy 32:35, God says, *"Vengeance is mine; I will repay."*) Yes ☐ No ☐

4. If a coworker was saying derogatory things about the boss, what would you do? _____
_____

5. If your spouse did not want you to attend religious services, would you go anyway? Yes ☐ No ☐

6. Name one spiritual boundary you need in your life. _____
_____

7. Do you find that it is becoming more difficult to take a stand for what you believe in today's society? Yes ☐ No ☐

Next Step: *"Love the Lord your God with all your heart and with all your soul and with all your strength"* (Deuteronomy 6:5). Prayerfully consider how well you are doing this in your life and what changes you need to make to better fulfill this command.

WEEK EIGHT
Fear

"Of all the liars in the world, sometimes the worst are our own fears."

\- Rudyard Kipling

Day One
Nothing to Fear

Ashlyn Blocker is a teenager who lives with her parents in Patterson, Georgia. She was born with a rare inherited condition that turns off the body's pain sensors. Only about one in a million people have the congenital condition of CIP. These individuals are at risk of severely injuring themselves from an early age and potentially causing premature death.

God has created our bodies to feel pain and fear danger. This is for our preservation. The Bible tells us we are to fear God. However, repeatedly in the Bible we are told to "fear not." That is because there are two kinds of fear. There are healthy fears and unhealthy fears.

When my son was small he attended a birthday party that included a bounce house. As the party was ending, he stepped on the electrical cord to the bounce house that was laying across a damp spot in the yard. When he did, he experienced a shock that shorted out the cord and deflated the bounce house. It was a terrifying experience. There was a small fray in the cord that left part of the electrical wire exposed. Fortunately, my son was not seriously hurt.

We depend on electricity, but it is a powerful force that can kill. We are wise to fear and respect it. Similarly, that is how we are to view God. He is all-loving but he is also all-powerful. He wants to have a loving relationship with each of us but he also wants us to fear and respect him. A fear of God, and things such as electricity, bombs, or a gun wielding madman are all healthy fears.

When we moved to Florida, we lived in an apartment for a couple of years before buying our house. One night, while getting ready for bed, I opened a drawer in the bathroom. A small roach ran out and I jumped back, slipped on a rug, fell forward into the edge of the cabinet which knocked me backwards against the edge of the tub and then I fell to the floor where I laid motionless. I thought my back was broken and I also had excruciating pain in my arm and hip. A trip to the ER and multiple x-rays later, I was relieved to find out that nothing was broken. In case you hadn't guessed, I have an unhealthy fear of roaches.

Fear is an unpleasant feeling triggered by the perception of danger, real or imagined. When the danger is real, that's a healthy fear. When it is imagined, it is unhealthy. An acrostic in that case is **F**alse **E**vidence **A**ppearing **R**eal. Our focus this week is on those unhealthy fears.

Day One Assignments

When you have been betrayed by the one person you love the most, it is understandable to experience a fear of a recurrence. That kind of trauma can introduce a host of fears such as fear of rejection, disease, inadequacy, abandonment, intimacy, and failure. Unfortunately, almost everyone enters marriage with some baggage from past trauma, wounds, or difficulties that is often stirred by the current situation.

1. Has your husband's sexual acting out triggered bad memories from your past? Yes □ No □ If so, what are they? _____

_____

_____

_____

2. With what fears are you now wrestling as a result of this current betrayal? _____

_____

_____

_____

3. On a scale of one to ten, with one being "rarely struggle with fear" and ten being "so fearful I can barely function," how much is fear a part of your life right now?

1   2   3   4   5   6   7   8   9   10

4. Name the one fear that most haunts you currently.

_____

5. On a continuum of one to ten, with one being a "strong unhealthy fear of God," five being "indifferent" to God, and ten being a healthy "strong fear and reverence" of God, where are you?

1   2   3   4   5   6   7   8   9   10

Next Step: Admit to God areas in which you are lacking in a healthy fear of him and areas in which you are struggling with unhealthy fears. Ask him to help you in both of those areas.

Day Two
Fear's Origin

A phobia is a persistent, excessive fear of an object or situation that produces such anxiety and panic that the individual will go to great lengths to avoid it. There are hundreds of phobias. According to the National Institute of Mental Health, approximately 10 percent of people in the U.S. have a specific phobia.

Common phobias include fear of flying, heights, public speaking, and spiders. There are some less common phobias that are interesting and even comical if they aren't yours: mysophobia, the fear of dirt; chaetophobia, fear of hairy people; odontophobia, fear of teeth; porphyrophobia, fear of the color purple; pogonophobia, fear of beards; and alektorophobia, the fear of chickens.

Fear is as old as mankind. Since God created us with a sense of healthy fears for our protection, that makes perfect sense. But unhealthy fear resulted from the fall of man. Genesis tells the story of the creation of man, whom God placed in the beautiful Garden of Eden with the instruction to him and his wife that they may enjoy every single thing there except the fruit of one tree.

They both ate of that one forbidden tree and their eyes were opened to the fact that they were naked. Even though there was nothing new about that fact, their disobedience to God's command caused them to feel shame, and they hid. When God called out to them, Genesis 3:10 says Adam responded, *"I heard you in the garden, I was afraid because I was naked; so I hid."* This is the very fear that causes the addict to hide his acting out. It is the shame that covers him and fear of exposure that leads him to lie. But he is not alone. That is an unhealthy fear that plagues all of us.

Let's look at how the physical body responds to fear. As we've seen, healthy fear is designed to protect us. To facilitate that, our bodies react to perceived threats to prepare us to fight, flee, or freeze. There is a release of hormones that slow down functions such as digestion that are not needed for immediate survival. Blood flow to the muscles increases, strengthening them to spring into action. The heart rate increases to pump that extra blood where it's needed. The increased heart rate in rabbits who perceive a threat can lead to a heart attack. It can do that in humans also.

Though the body was wonderfully designed to respond to fear from danger, for our survival, remaining in a fearful state can have many negative effects on us. We will address those effects tomorrow.

Day Two Assignments

Moses led the children of Israel through the wilderness for 40 years with Joshua by his side the entire time. The plan was for them both to enter the Promised Land with God's people. During one of the many times the people were complaining, this time for water, Moses cried out to God for help, as he usually did. God instructed Moses to speak to a rock to bring forth water. But in Moses' frustration with the people, he struck the rock with his staff as he spoke to it. Water came forth, but because Moses had not followed God's instructions, God told him he would not enter the Promised Land with the others.

Moses died and God appointed Joshua as the new leader. The responsibility then fell on him to lead God's people into battle as they entered the Promised Land. There were many battles to follow to secure the land and Joshua never imagined he would be doing this without Moses. Naturally, he felt great fear.

God understood that fear and repeatedly encouraged Joshua as he did in Joshua 1:9 when he said, *"Be strong and courageous. Do not be afraid; do not be discouraged, for the Lord your God will be with you wherever you go."*

The man who has been by your side for years, also failed to follow God's commands. Now you are traveling a road you never anticipated and your future may seem unclear. Whether you are no longer with your spouse or things are just uncertain for now, God still has a Promised Land for you. He still has great things in store for your future. The same encouragement he gave to Joshua he gives to you. Precious lady, don't be afraid or discouraged. He will strengthen you and walk with you every step of the way, through the battles and on to victory.

1. Do you fear that your future may be doomed because of your husband's poor choices? Yes ☐ No ☐

2. Are you fearful of facing a future without your spouse? Yes ☐ No ☐

3. Do you think God is any less powerful today than he was when he equipped, strengthened, and led Joshua? Yes □ No □

Next Step: Ask God to give you a fresh vision for a great future. Depend on his strength and presence to lead you there.

Day Three
The Effects of Fear

When God gives us a command, it is not to punish us or keep us from having a good time. It is for our own good. When he repeatedly tells us not to fear, he does so because he wants us to trust in him and because he knows such fear is detrimental to us. The physical effects of fear caused by a real danger prepare us for action. But staying in a state of unhealthy fear is harmful.

You send the message to your body that fear is present and your body cannot distinguish whether it is real or not. It responds the same either way. Hormones are released and heart rate and blood flow increase. Since our bodies were not designed to stay in that perpetual state, they will be negatively impacted in many ways. Here are just some of those effects:

On the body

- Weakens immune system

- Damages cardiovascular and gastrointestinal systems

- Fatigue

On the mind

- Impairs memory

- Slows brain processing and reactivity

- Unregulated emotions

- Depression

- Impulsive behavior

On the spirit

- Doubt God

- Blame God

- Withdraw from God

On others

- Isolates

- Contagious

Day Three Assignments

Saul was anointed the first king of Israel. He had a bright future but his fears sabotaged that. On one occasion, God commanded Saul to lead his people to conquer an enemy and spare nothing and no one. Instead, he spared the king and kept the best of the spoils. When confronted by the priest, he admitted that he disobeyed the instructions out of fear. *"Saul said to Samuel, 'I have sinned, I have violated the Lord's command and your instructions. I was afraid of the men and so I gave in to them'"* (I Samuel 15:24).

Later, King Saul became afraid of David because the Lord was with David but had left him (I Samuel 18:12). During one episode, Saul was so overtaken with this fear that he hurled a spear at David in an attempt to pin him to a wall and kill him. King Saul continued to pursue David despite David's loyalty to him. Saul became completely irrational due to his fear.

I've known people who had health issues but wouldn't go to the doctor out of a fear that they might have something seriously wrong. Out of fear of losing their husbands, some women go to extremes to change their looks through crazy dieting, obsessive exercising or even plastic surgery in ways they think will make themselves more attractive and desirable.

Living in fear can harm us – body, mind, and spirit – as well as negatively impact our relationships with those around us. In the case of King Saul, ongoing fear led to unregulated emotions and impulsive behavior causing him to act in crazy and illogical ways.

1. Have you experienced negative physical effects on your body due to ongoing fears? Yes ☐ No ☐ If so, how? _____
_____
_____

2. Has fear caused you to be forgetful or sluggish in your thinking?
Yes ☐ No ☐

3. Has fear caused you to do or consider doing anything extreme to attempt to make your spouse more attracted to you? Yes ☐ No ☐

4. Has fear caused you to doubt, blame, or withdraw from God?
Yes ☐ No ☐

5. Have you isolated yourself, either physically or emotionally, out of fear of being hurt? Yes ☐ No ☐

Next Step: Be honest about the level of fear you are experiencing and the negative impact it is having on you. Confess that to God and to a safe person.

Day Four
Escape to Nowhere

Fear can slow our brain functioning and hamper our reasoning, so it is no surprise that we often cope with fear in destructive ways. Facing our fears can be frightening, but denying or ignoring them is unproductive and harmful. Robert Frost said, "The best way out is through." That is certainly true when dealing with fear.

Here are a few poor coping mechanisms for dealing with fear.

1. Approval Seeking

Fear can be contagious. When dealing with fear, we tend to exaggerate the narratives playing through our minds. Then we look for others to validate what we fear. The old saying, "Misery loves company" applies here.

The Bible tells the story of Moses sending 12 spies to check out the Promised Land that God was sending them into. Ten of the men came back agreeing that the land was indeed beautiful and abundant. But their focus on the giants in the land led them to conclude that they could not achieve victory against them. When they reported it to the hundreds of thousands of people back in the camp, they played up the danger. Soon, the overwhelming majority affirmed their fears and refused to advance.

The wisest thing we can do when battling fear is to surround ourselves with a few positive people who will help us to see things in the proper perspective.

2. Distraction through caretaking

While temporary distractions can give us a needed break from overwhelming thoughts, maintaining a lifestyle of distraction is unhealthy. This occurs when we turn all of our energy into helping others with their problems. Again, taking a break to help someone else can get us out of our self-centeredness and give us a fresh perspective about our own issues. But caretaking as a means of escape is unhealthy.

3. Isolating

Fear of being hurt, or other relational fears, can lead us to isolate. The thinking is that if we keep people at a distance, they can't hurt us. The prophet Elijah, when he was running in fear from the evil Jezebel, went by himself into the desert and later to a cave. But isolating can lead to loneliness and can make us more vulnerable to negative thinking. Elijah, from the mouth of the cave, told God that he was the only prophet of the Lord left on the earth and he accused God of trying to kill him. That story is a great example of isolation leading to extreme and negative thinking. *"The Lord God said, 'It is not good for the man to be alone'"* (Genesis 2:18).

4. Medicating

When fear becomes overwhelming, there is often great temptation to escape the pain by partaking in something that makes us feel better. Some turn to alcohol or drugs. Others may overeat or overspend. Extreme anger can be an escape for others. Anything that causes a release of endorphins, which numbs pain and leads to feelings of euphoria, can eventually lead to addiction. If I occasionally have a piece of chocolate or a hot fudge sundae to make me feel better, that is one thing. But if I regularly try to escape feelings of fear by turning to a substance or activity, that is an unhealthy coping mechanism that will likely have detrimental long-term effects.

5. Obsessing over worst case scenarios

Edmund Burke said, "Fears are stories we tell ourselves." When we are plagued with unhealthy fear, often at the root of it we'll find faulty and extreme thinking. Rarely do I speak to a woman experiencing the trauma caused by sexual betrayal, who paints best case scenario pictures for me. Granted, there can be many unknowns in families affected by porn and sex addiction. And not knowing what to expect makes most of us uneasy. Teal Swan said, "We do not fear the unknown. We fear what we think we know about the unknown." We can train ourselves to imagine positive futures and maintain our peace and serenity, or we can continue to ruminate on disastrous scenarios and forfeit our peace and our health.

Day Four Assignments

"That day when evening came, he (Jesus) said to his disciples, 'Let us go over to the other side.' Leaving the crowd behind, they took him along, just as he was, in the boat. There were also other boats with him. A furious squall came up, and the waves broke over the boat, so that it was nearly swamped. Jesus was in the stern, sleeping on a cushion. The disciples woke him and said to him, 'Teacher, don't you care if we drown?'

He got up, rebuked the wind and said to the waves, 'Quiet! Be still!' Then the wind died down and it was completely calm.

He said to his disciples, 'Why are you so afraid? Do you still have no faith?'" (Mark 4:35-40).

The disciples, filled with fear, not only forgot that Jesus had promised that they were going to the other side of the lake, they also forgot all of the great things they had seen him do before. In their fear, they even accused Jesus of not caring if they drowned. They clearly weren't going to get an "A" for how they coped with fear in that test.

In the fallout of betrayal, has fear caused you to forget all the times God brought you through tough times in the past? Like the disciples, have you questioned if God even cares about what you are going through?

Take a few minutes to remember past difficult situations in your life and how God brought you through them. Write a few of them down. _____

_____

_____

_____

Aristotle said, "Fear is pain arising from the anticipation of evil." Do you anticipate only negative things in your future? A study indicates 85 percent of what people worried about never happened and of the 15 percent that did happen, 79 percent of the people said they handled it better than they imagined they would. Sixteenth century French writer and philosopher Michel de Montaigne said, "My life has been filled with terrible misfortune; most of which never happened."

Do you tend to spend your time imagining worst case scenarios for your future? Yes □ No □

Consider two scenarios that you have been tempted to imagine turning out the worst. Write down how those would look if they turned out the best. _____
_____
_____

Next Step: Refuse to respond to fear in unhealthy ways. Imagine how much more peace would fill your life if you would begin to think about the best possible scenarios for your future instead of the worst. Ask God to help you change your way of thinking.

Day Five
Consider the Source

"For God has not given us a spirit of fear, but of power, and of love, and of a sound mind" (2 Timothy 1:7 NKJV).

Those nagging, unhealthy fears tormenting your thinking are not from God. When we are filled with fear, we feel weak and vulnerable. God gives us a spirit of power. When we are afraid, we tend to withdraw and isolate. God gives us love so we'll connect with others. When we continually obsess with trepidation, we don't think clearly. God gives us a sound mind. We have a choice. We can accept the fear the enemy holds out to us or we can accept the power, love and sound mind God offers us. Which do you choose?

I remember when I was in school, occasionally the teacher would bring in a projector for a presentation. The light would shine on the material and then greatly enlarge it and project it onto a large screen or a wall so all could see. Inevitably, some child would hold his hand to form the shape of a rabbit's head and ears or the head of a dog and hold it in front of the light. It appeared on the wall to be a giant rabbit or dog.

When we experience trauma, our tendency is to shine the spotlight on our problems such that they are magnified and projected ever before us, casting haunting images that hang over us, threatening everything we hold dear. But we can instead choose to shine the light of God's presence on our fears and watch them shrink. How do we do that practically?

1. Identify the fear.

It is difficult to battle an unknown enemy. When the feelings of uneasiness and fear start gripping us, it is best to pause and ask, "What am I feeling and why am I feeling this way? Of what exactly am I afraid?" Name it.

2. Recognize the source.

There is a chance that there is a real danger. Certainly this would be true in the case of an abusive spouse. More often than not though, there are unhealthy fears at play, threatening to steal our peace – a tactic of the enemy.

3. Admit the fear.

Just as sexual addiction thrives in darkness, fears do as well. Something amazing happens when we admit our fears to God and someone else. They begin to feel less scary because we begin to feel less alone in the battle. Living alone in our fear is not God's plan. *"Confess your faults one to another, and pray one for another, that you may be healed"* (James 5:16 NKJV).

4. Breathe.

As we already read this week, when fear grips us, our bodies respond to prepare us for action. Elevated heart rate and tensed muscles are two of those responses. That in itself can cause us to feel anxious. It is beneficial to take slow, deep breaths and to concentrate on relaxing the muscles and slowing down the heart rate.

5. Pray.

"Be anxious for nothing, but in everything by prayer and supplication with thanksgiving let your requests be made known to God. And the peace of God, which surpasses all comprehension, will guard your hearts and your minds in Christ Jesus" (Philippians 4:6-7 NASB).

6. Imagine the best case scenario.

As we saw yesterday, our natural tendency is to allow our minds to dwell on the worst possible outcomes. Instead, imagine and journal about the best possible outcome. Dwelling on the negative feeds fears. Dwelling on the positive feeds faith. *"Surely the righteous will never be shaken; they will be remembered forever. They will have no fear of bad news; their hearts are steadfast, trusting in the Lord"* (Psalm 112:6-7). Fear and faith both ask us to believe in something we can't see but only one of those leads to peace.

7. Prepare.

If fear can be eased by doing something in our control, we are wise to do it. If a mom fears she might not be able to provide for her children if her spouse doesn't choose recovery, going back to work, taking a class, or doing something to improve her skills are things she can do that might help her feel more prepared and alleviate her fears.

8. Maintain proper perspective.

The same God who gave us the instinct to perceive danger and respond, tells us repeatedly to fear not. Why? It is not because there aren't occasionally real dangers, though the majority of things we fear are scenarios we make up in our minds that never happen. It is because the power of any real danger pales in comparison to the power of an almighty God.

Focus on the size of your God, not the size of your fear.

Day Five Assignments

When I am home alone and it is dark outside, if I hear a noise while I'm lying in bed with the lights off, sometimes it frightens me. But if I'm in my house in the middle of the afternoon and someone else is with me, if I hear the same noise, it might get my attention but it is not likely to evoke fear.

Similarly, when we are feeling fear, if we acknowledge it and tell someone else about it, it loses much of its power. Mark Burnett said, "Facing your fears robs them of their power."

Write the name of one person with whom you can share your fears. __

_____

Call, text, or email that person this week and share your current worst fear.

Prepare for your next battle with fear by writing down a few things you can read and repeat to yourself when the time comes. It could be encouraging sayings, positive self-talk or Bible verses.

Here are a few examples:

> I won't let fear decide my future.
> Fear is a story I tell myself and so I choose to tell myself a different story.
> I am brave. I am strong.
> Fear will not rule my life anymore.
> *"I trust in God, so why should I be afraid? What can mere mortals do to me?"* (Psalm 56:4).
> *"I sought the Lord, and he answered me; he delivered me from all my fears"* (Psalm 34:4).

_____
_____
_____
_____

Next Step: We can feed our faith or feed our fears. The one most nourished wins. Commit to feeding your faith and then do it.

WEEK NINE
Worthwhile

"It is not the mountain we conquer, but ourselves."

\- Sir Edmund Hillary

Day One
Devalued

Time-lapse photography allows us to view changes at a normal speed that would otherwise take an extended period to visualize. I believe if we could capture the typical deterioration of the self-esteem of a sex addict's spouse through time-lapse photography, it would be heartbreaking. For most of these partners, this is a slow, chipping away process until the ultimate discovery unleashes a wrecking ball on her already eroding sense of self-worth.

This decline may be due to the wounded spouse's perception that something is causing her husband to pull away or it may be the direct result of the criticism and blame he's heaped upon her to justify his acting out. Either way, it is rare for a woman's sense of value to not be adversely affected by her husband's behavior, whether she knows yet of his addiction or not.

So what is self-worth and from where is it derived? Self-worth, often used interchangeably with self-esteem, is the valuing of your inherent worth as a person. For many people, this is measured by others' opinions of them, the standards of their society, and their view of their own accomplishments.

In America, a high premium is placed on physical appearance, financial resources, academic achievement, career performance, and other such things. We also live in a time when images and messages touting sexuality, sexual prowess, and satisfaction bombard us. This leaves the individual who determines his or her value by societal messages on shaky ground, much like the foolish man spoken of in Matthew 7:26 who built his house upon the sand.

With this measuring stick, the wounded spouse will likely experience a drop in her self-worth, especially when she is struggling with feeling unlovable, unattractive, and unwanted. Society imparts a message that if there is something wrong with your marital relationship, there is something wrong with you. Unfortunately, this may be reinforced if the wife sees an uninformed therapist or pastor who advises her to be more sexual with her partner and satisfy his needs in order to solve the problem.

However, a woman with a healthy sense of self-worth, one that is not dependent on the opinion of others, personal achievements, or other external factors, better weathers the storm of betrayal. She is able to internalize the truth that her husband's poor choices have nothing to do with her, regardless of his statements to the contrary. Eleanor Roosevelt said, "No one can make you feel inferior without your consent."

This week we will look at the birth and foundation of healthy self-worth and how to recover yours if it has been damaged by your husband's sexual addiction.

Day One Assignments

If I get a brand new, crisp $100 bill from the bank, I know that bill is worth $100. But, what if I tear off a corner of that bill, crumple it, throw it on the ground and drag it through the mud? Who would want it then? What if every other person said it wasn't worth anything anymore? How much is it now worth? It is still worth $100. Why? Since the U.S. Department of Treasury makes the money, only they can set its value. I can't take a $1 bill to Macy's and successfully buy a dress by telling the clerk I've determined the bill is worth $100 any more than someone can change the worth of my $100 bill by saying it is now worth only $1.

Precious lady, you may have been trampled by the sexual addiction of your spouse, but it does not devalue you in any way. His problem says nothing about you as a wife. In fact, it has nothing to do with you at all. It is not personal, even though it feels *very* personal. Unfortunately, it can be difficult to connect our heads with our hearts on this one.

Take a minute to answer the following questions to help you consider the health of your sense of self-worth.

1. Are you extremely critical of yourself?
2. Do you downplay or ignore your positive qualities?
3. Do you use negative words to describe yourself, such as stupid, fat, ugly, or unlovable?
4. Do you judge yourself to be inferior to your peers?
5. Do you have difficulty believing a person who compliments you?
6. Do you blame yourself when things go wrong instead of taking into account things over which you have no control?
7. Do you feel devastated when someone criticizes you?
8. Do you feel like you regularly let other people down?
9. Do you feel like your life is insignificant?
10. Do you worry about what other people think about you?

I've discovered that it is not uncommon to think we have a fairly healthy sense of our value as individuals until we consider questions like those above. We then may realize that there is definitely room for improvement.

Next Step: Admit to God any struggle you have believing you have infinite value as his child. Ask him to help you stop using the world's criteria as your standard.

Day Two
Nature vs. Nurture

Children are born with great self-esteem. They are totally reliant on others and don't seem to mind. They are not bashful in expressing their needs and are apparently unconcerned with how they are perceived. They are completely comfortable in their own skin with no hint of self-consciousness. So, why don't they all grow into healthy, self-confident adults?

In 1943, American Psychologist Abraham Maslow introduced what he called the hierarchy of needs. His theory was that at the bottom of the pyramid were basic physiological needs of food, water, and warmth. As long as these needs were met, an individual was basically happy and fulfilled. Next was the need for security. Using Maslow's theory, it is understandable why most children, especially those born in industrialized countries, have healthy self-esteem since most have those basic physiological needs met.

However, according to Maslow's pyramid of needs, next need is for love. This is when children may begin experiencing things that chip away at their self-esteem. If a child has an emotionally unavailable, abusive, critical, or neglecting parent, this can lead to insecurity and poor self-esteem.

Another cause of low self-esteem can be having teachers, coaches, or other influencers in life, who are not affirming. These are usually individuals who spend a great deal of time with a child and whom they are taught to respect. There are thousands of stories of adults who can vividly remember the stinging words of one teacher who told them things such as they would never amount to anything or that they'd never be successful.

When I wore a black dress to school one day, I will never forget my high school calculus teacher telling me that blondes wearing black look like sluts. Those types of remarks stick with impressionable young people and can cause real emotional damage.

Traumatic life events can also affect self-esteem. It is not uncommon for the child who has lost a parent through death or divorce to experience a fear of abandonment and to develop a false narrative that those he loves eventually leave. This can damage self-esteem well into adulthood, especially without extensive therapy to counter this distorted message.

Someone experiencing ongoing medical issues might have limitations that adversely affect self-esteem. Depression, whether as a result of those health issues or something else, can damage a person's sense of worth. This can be compounded by the stigma that unfortunately still surrounds depression.

Ongoing poor treatment from a spouse, due to sexual addiction or other issues can negatively impact a woman's sense of her value. And if she is already inclined to believe there is something wrong with her due to past experiences in her life, this treatment from her husband compounds the problem.

A healthy immune system doesn't guarantee you'll never become ill, but it does reduce your susceptibility to illness and can improve your odds for a speedy recovery if you do get sick. Likewise, a healthy self-esteem doesn't guarantee that a woman experiencing betrayal trauma will never struggle from a lack of confidence or that she'll never feel inferior or unworthy, but it does lessen the likelihood that she will fall into that trap, and if she does, she is more likely to get back on her feet quickly.

Day Two Assignments

1. Do you remember feeling self-confident and secure as a child?
Yes □ No □

2. As a child, was there ever a time when your basic physical needs were not met? Yes □ No □

3. Did you feel a close emotional bond with your parents while growing up? Yes □ No □

4. Did you ever have a teacher or other influential person in your childhood who said or did something that caused you to feel inferior to others? Yes □ No □ If yes, explain. _____
_____
_____

5. Did you have any events in your childhood that you felt were traumatic? Yes □ No □ If so, explain. _____
_____
_____
_____

6. Do you have anything else in your past that you feel negatively impacted your sense of self-worth? Yes □ No □ If so, explain. _____
_____
_____
_____

We can't change our past, but we don't have to allow it to define us. God can take all of our life experiences, good and bad, and weave together a beautiful tapestry. *"And we know that God causes everything to work together for the good of those who love God and are called according to his purpose for them"* (Romans 8:28 NLT).

Next Step: Surrender any negative childhood experiences to God and ask him to relieve any pain you've been carrying from them. Ask him to help you see how he can redeem those events for good.

Day Three
Standardized Test

I'm considering having some new flooring installed. To get an idea of how much it may cost, I measured the area and took those measurements to the store where I picked out the flooring and presented all of that information to the salesman. Now imagine if on my measuring tape, 12 inches equaled a foot but when I got the the store, their tape measure had 10 inches equaling a foot. For one thing, I'd be upset because the new flooring would cost me more money. Who gets to determine which measurement is correct?

That is part of the problem with basing our self-worth on the standards of the world. Is there just one standard out there? Who determines that standard? Is it fixed or does it change? Are there different standards in different parts of the world?

If I ask you if you are rich, you would likely tell me, "No." Most people would probably respond the same. But what is your standard? Rich compared to whom? Over a billion people in the world live on less than $1 per day. Compared to the rest of the world, most of us would be considered rich. Are you beautiful? Again, the answer depends on the standard you use and where in the world you live. Standards of beauty vary.

The problem with determining our inner self-worth by external criteria is that we must have others for comparison to determine a value. Getting into the comparison trap seldom leads to anything good. If I compare myself to someone else, I am likely to determine I don't measure up and therefore I feel badly about myself or I determine I come out ahead and I feel like I'm better than that person.

One danger with determining someone's worth by external markers is seen in how some arbitrary value can taint one person's view of another. If I place a high value on thinness, I run the risk of seeing someone overweight and making an assumption that it says something about his or her character. I might conclude that person is lazy or unmotivated.

No, our worth is not determined by external things. All humans have inherent value as a creation of an almighty God. But it goes a step further. God created animals, plants and trees, but they don't have our value. We are the only creation made in his image. *"God created man in his own image; in the image of God he created him; male and female he created them"* (Genesis 1:27 NASB).

We are created and loved by the God of the universe. He is our standard. He is consistent and his love is eternal. He loves us not because of anything we have done but because we are his children. There is nothing we can do to make God loves us more and there is nothing we can do to make him love us less. *"I have loved you with an everlasting love; therefore, I have continued my faithfulness to you"* (Jeremiah 31:3 ESV). That alone is our standardized test.

Day Three Assignments

God instructed Samuel the priest to go to the house of Jesse and to anoint one of his sons to whom God would direct him to, so he could become the next king of Israel in place of King Saul who had disobeyed God. The Bible said Saul was an impressive looking, tall and handsome man. Samuel may have thought those were necessary qualities for a king because when he saw Jesse's son Eliab, he apparently looked the part and Samuel concluded he must be the next king. *"But the Lord said to Samuel, 'Do not consider his appearance or his height, for I have rejected him. The Lord does not look at the things people look at. People look at the outward appearance, but the Lord looks at the heart'"* (I Samuel 16:7).

We live in a world that values external things such as appearance, achievements, and material possessions. But what we accomplish, what we possess, and how we look don't define who we are or what we are worth.

1. Have you fallen into the comparison trap? Does your self-esteem fluctuate depending on how you think you compare to others?
Yes ☐ No ☐

2. Do you tend to judge others' insides by external things? Yes ☐ No ☐

3. Have you ever judged someone by external factors and later discovered they were very different than you had surmised? Yes ☐ No ☐

4. Do you gauge your value as an individual by past experiences, successes, or failures? Yes ☐ No ☐

5. How would your opinion of your self-worth change if you could consistently remember that your value is based solely on your position as a child of God? Explain. _____
_____
_____
_____

Next Step: God looks past our outward appearance and accomplishments and looks at our heart. Ask God to help you to look at yourself and others as he does.

Day Four
Balancing Act

"Love your neighbor as yourself" (Matthew 22:39). It is easy to look at this verse and see that we are to love our neighbor. That is a command from God. Does it also tell us to love ourselves? Jesus actually said this is the second great command likened to the command to love God with all we are. But it did not say it was the second and third command. It is our human nature to put ourselves first. We are self-centered from birth.

This verse does not tell us to not love ourselves. Again, the focus is on others. This verse is not the crux of the reason we are to have a healthy sense of self-worth. As we saw yesterday, our value is based only on the fact that we are created in the image of God. That, coupled with the unconditional, everlasting love of the Father, should be the basis for our self-esteem.

While we are to value ourselves, we are not to value ourselves more than we value others. *"Do not think of yourself more highly than you ought, but rather think of yourself with sober judgment, in accordance with the faith God has distributed to each of you"* (Romans 12:3). We are not superior to any other person. Nor are we inferior to any other person. We are all equal under God.

Each of us is a unique creation with different gifts, talents, and attributes. While our value is not determined by our accomplishments, God did give us these different talents with the instruction to use them. The fact that God's love for us is unconditional does not absolve us of our calling to honor him and help others with the abilities with which we've been entrusted.

When we discover that we are married to sex addicts, it is easy to focus on their mistakes and failures. Rather than allowing that to consume us, we will benefit more from looking at our own character defects and shortcomings. No one is perfect. Please understand, I am not saying any of your imperfections justify your husband's sexual acting out. They do not. But no one is perfect.

We all have room to grow. By turning your attention to discovering and removing your own defects, you will become an overall healthier person, and you may develop more compassion and understanding for your spouse.

We are to recognize that we have incredible worth, not because of what we've accomplished or attained but because we are unconditionally loved children of God. But we are no better than anyone else. We are to love and value others as well. We are also called to use the gifts and talents God has bestowed upon us and to allow God to mold our character to be more like him. Finding the proper balance for all of that is not easy. We need God's wisdom and direction to pull that off. Thomas Kinkade said, "Balance, peace, and joy are the fruit of a successful life. It starts with recognizing your talents and finding ways to serve others by using them."

Day Four Assignments

As we've seen this week, our sense of self-worth should be strong and secure regardless of our accomplishments or failures, despite the opinions of others, and no matter what we've experienced. Though our value as individuals is not dependent upon this, we should consider how well we are using the talents and abilities we've been given and what character defects we have that are standing in the way of us honoring God in all areas of our lives. *"Let us examine our ways and test them, and let us return to the Lord"* (Lamentations 3:40).

1. Name one talent (innate ability) you have. _____

2. How are you using that talent? _____
_____

3. Name one character defect you know you should surrender to God.
_____

4. Name one mistake you tend to repeatedly make. _____
_____

5. What are the qualities you value? _____
_____

6. Do you spend more time developing those qualities in your own life or focusing on the external things you think others are more likely to notice? _____
_____

7. Who inspires you and why? _____
_____

Next Step: Take some time to consider your character defects. Confess and surrender them to God. Thank him that though he loves you in spite of them, he has made his power available to you to overcome them if you submit to him.

Day Five
Self-Esteem Boosters

We should know by Day Five that we aren't to rely on others to provide us with a sense of self-worth. As a matter of fact, what others think of us is none of our business. That is their issue and we can't control it. We are fully known and fully loved by God just as we are. Abraham Lincoln said, "It is difficult to make a man miserable while he feels worth of himself and claims kindred to the great God who made him."

But the reality is that current or past relationships with partners who have a porn or sexual addiction can do a number on your self-esteem. If this is true of you, how do you undo that damage? How do you change your negative thinking about yourself?

1. Remind yourself that your worth comes from God.

"For you created my inmost being; you knit me together in my mother's womb. I praise you because I am fearfully and wonderfully made; your works are wonderful, I know that full well" (Psalm 139:13-14).

2. Speak kindly to yourself.

Would you talk to others you love the way you talk to yourself? Encourage yourself as you would a child who is doing her best.

3. Challenge negative self-talk.

How often we get frustrated and angry when we make a mistake and say things to ourselves such as, "You never do anything right! You're such an idiot!" Are those statements really true? Consider replacing such statements with something like, "I blew it this time but I can do better next time."

4. Don't compare yourself to others.

The reality is no two people are the same and no two situations are the same. People tend to put forth the image of themselves they want others to see when who they really are may be quite different.

5. Acknowledge your positive qualities.

Are you kind? Are you a loyal friend? Are you creative? We all have gifts, talents, and skills of some kind.

6. Let go of past hurts and mistakes.

Learn from them and move on. Hanging onto them is like carrying around rotten garbage. The smell permeates and spoils everything around it.

7. Be assertive. Make your own decisions.

Take part in things you think are important. Speak up for what you believe and what you need. Express your opinions. You are worthy of love and respect.

8. Take care of yourself.

Don't wait for others to do it for you. You are capable and you deserve it. You can't fulfill your destiny if you don't take care of yourself.

Henry Ford said, "Whether you think you can or think you can't – you are right."

Day Five Assignments

You are God's masterpiece. A masterpiece is a person's greatest work of art.

1. Write one Bible verse that speaks of your worth on an index card or slip of paper and place it on your bathroom mirror. Here are three examples in case you need help.

"So God created man in his own image; in the image of God he created him; male and female he created them" (Genesis 1:27 NASB).

"For you created my inmost being; you knit me together in my mother's womb. I praise you because I am fearfully and wonderfully made; your works are wonderful, I know that full well" (Psalm 139:13-14).

"See what great love the Father has lavished on us, that we should be called children of God! And that is what we are!" (I John 3:1).

2. Begin each day by saying one positive thing to yourself in the mirror.

3. Replace negative self-talk with a healthier reality. (Replace a phrase like, "I always screw up" with something like, "I messed up this time but I'll do better next time.")

4. List three of your positive qualities. _____
_____
_____

5. Name one mistake you made in the past year and something you learned from it. _____
_____
_____
_____

6. Do one thing special for yourself this week. (Go for a walk, have lunch with a friend, get a pedicure.)

7. Make a point to share a feeling, need, or opinion with someone this week. Record it here. _____

_____

_____

Next Step: The God who knows you best, loves you most simply because you are his prized creation. Focus on that thought this week and live like you believe it.

WEEK TEN
Good Grief

"We can endure much more than we think we can: all human experience testifies to that. All we need to do is learn not to be afraid of pain. Grit your teeth and let it hurt. Don't deny it, don't be overwhelmed by it. It will not last forever. One day, the pain will be gone and you will still be there."

- Rabbi Harold Kushner,

When All You've Ever Wanted Isn't Enough

Day One
The Unwanted Gift of Grief

No little girl grows up thinking, "One day I want to marry a sex addict," and very few women would marry a man whom she knew already to be one. Most of us enter marriage with hearts full of love and minds full of dreams for our future. Many of us stand before our family, friends, and God and pledge our love and commitment to our partners, with the promise to forsake all others. Later, when the one we trusted most destroys that trust by way of sexual betrayal, the floodgate of grief is opened.

Grief is a deep and poignant distress caused by the loss of someone or something important. Intense sorrow and sadness are normal responses to such loss. But in a society where a high premium is placed on happiness, grief is not only unwelcome, it is often avoided.

Grief is unavoidable and universal. No one in this world is spared. Why would a loving God allow such misery? *Jesus said, 'Blessed are those who mourn, for they will be comforted'"* (Matthew 5:4). Those who grieve have the opportunity to experience God in a powerful and life transforming way. C.S. Lewis said it like this: "Pain insists upon being attended to. God whispers to us in our pleasures, speaks in our consciences, but shouts in our pains. It is his megaphone to rouse a deaf world." It can be God's reminder that there is more to life than what we see and experience in this world; that we are spiritual beings with an eternal future beyond this life.

Grief, though all-inclusive, is unique. People grieve in various ways that are influenced by their culture, upbringing, and personality. In 1969, in her book *On Death and Dying*, Elisabeth Kubler-Ross introduced the five stages of grief experienced by terminally ill patients. Though this became a widely applied framework, there are many who don't believe the grieving phases follow such a linear path, nor do they believe these stages necessarily apply to all types of grief. Before her death in 2004, the author said she "never meant to tuck messy emotions into a neat package."

Though not every individual will progress through the author's proposed five stages sequentially, or even go through all five of them at all, I believe they are experienced widely enough to be mentioned. The five stages of grief are denial, anger, bargaining, depression, and acceptance. Let's look at how someone facing the grief caused by betrayal trauma may experience each of these stages.

When a woman discovers her husband is a porn or sex addict, she will likely feel shocked and numb. This can serve to protect her from the overwhelming feelings that can accompany this discovery. In the first stage of grief, following the Kubler-Ross model, this woman may deny her spouse is really a sex addict or she may minimize the severity of the problem. As she begins to accept reality, anger can set in as she may blame God, her spouse's parents, his boss, circumstances, or her spouse for the problem. Her anger may even be directed at others with whom she may interact, who have nothing to do with the problem.

The bargaining phase may involve the wife trying to become more of what she thinks her husband desires in an attempt to "cure" his problem. She may believe if she were sexier, more available, or a better wife, he wouldn't look elsewhere to have his sexual needs met. When the realization dawns on her that there is nothing she can do to control her husband's addiction, she may become depressed. This will often lead to isolation.

The final stage of grief is acceptance. For the wife of a sex addict, this may be when she comes to understand that her husband has a problem that she cannot manage or fix and that her life will never be the same. Hopefully, even in her grief, she can believe God for a better future. Dr. Martin Luther King Jr. said, "When our days become dreary with low-hovering clouds of despair, and when our nights become darker than a thousand midnights, let us remember that there is a creative force in this universe, working to pull down the gigantic mountains of evil, a power that is able to make a way out of no way and transform dark yesterdays into bright tomorrows."

Day One Assignments

In Week 5 we looked at the role fear can play in masking pain and sadness. Writer James Baldwin said it this way: "I imagine one of the reasons people cling to their hate so stubbornly is because they sense, once hate is gone, they will be forced to deal with pain." At some point, we move beyond the anger, face the grief, and work through it.

King Solomon said, *"For everything there is a season, and a time for every matter under heaven: a time to weep and a time to laugh, a time to mourn and a time to dance"* (Ecclesiastes 3:1, 4 ESV). We suppress, postpone, and avoid grief because we don't want to feel the inevitable pain that comes from processing it. But Sigmund Freud said, "One day, in retrospect, the years of struggle will strike you as the most beautiful." Elisabeth Kubler-Ross said it like this: "Should you shield the valleys from the windstorms, you would never see the beauty of their canyons." There is beauty on the other side of grief. But you have to go through it to see it.

1. When growing up, how accepted were expressions of sadness and grief in your family? Explain. _____
_____
_____
_____

2. Of Elisabeth Kubler-Ross' five stages of grief (denial, anger, bargaining, depression, and acceptance), which ones have you experienced and how did they manifest in your life? _____
_____
_____
_____
_____
_____

3. Have you felt stuck anywhere in the grieving process? Yes ☐ No ☐

4. Have you intentionally taken time to grieve the losses you've experienced due to your husband's sexual acting out? Yes ☐ No ☐

Next Step: *"Weeping may last through the night, but joy comes with the morning"* (Psalm 30:5 NLT). There is joy to be found again on the other side of grief. Ask God to give you the strength to thoroughly embrace the grieving process so you can experience the healing and joy on the other side.

Day Two
Why and How We Avoid Grief

I don't imagine there is any healthy person who enjoys grief. But a person who avoids grieving will likely forfeit emotional health. So, other than the obvious goal of avoiding pain, why else might someone avoid grieving?

Why We Avoid Grief

1. How we were raised

"Stop crying or I'll give you something to cry about!" "Be a big girl and stop crying." "You don't want your friends to see you crying, do you?" "It's time to dry those tears and move on." These are just a few examples of how some families deal with emotions of sadness and grief. People who have been raised in such environments are taught that those feelings are not to be expressed, thus making it difficult to embrace them as adults.

2. Need to appear strong

Some believe that to be overcome with grief makes them look weak. Others may believe it shows a lack of spirituality. A parent may be hesitant to grieve, believing he or she must be strong for the children.

3. Alone

Part of the grieving process requires including others. It is difficult to completely grieve alone. When a mate is lost to death, it may be announced in the paper and on social media, usually resulting in an outpouring of love and support. A woman who has experienced betrayal seldom announces it on Facebook nor widely broadcasts the information. She may only tell a couple of people, if anyone. And those she does tell may not know how to come alongside her in her grief. This leaves her with no one with whom she can share her grief.

4. Shame

It is common for the spouse of a sex addict to feel shame. It is also common, even for well-meaning people, to not reach out to someone who has experienced pain, because they do not know what to say or they fear they might say the wrong thing. Unfortunately, this can feed the shame narrative the wounded spouse is already playing in her mind, leading her to questions such as "What's wrong with me?"

5. Myth that time will heal

Some individuals do not explore and embrace grief due to the false belief that time alone will eventually extinguish the pain and bring healing. But ignored grief is like a cancer. Though you may not be able to see it, it is on the inside, growing and causing damage that left unaddressed will eventually demand attention. The English hymn writer William Cowper said, "Grief is itself medicine." There can be no healing apart from it.

6. Lack of time

When the marital crisis of betrayal erupts, the world does not stand still. If it were the death of the loved one, the grieving spouse would typically be given time off from work. But with the discovery of sexual addiction, even in her pain, the grieving party is often expected to continue working, paying the bills, taking care of the children and the house, leaving little time to sit and process the grief she's experiencing.

Ways We Avoid the Grief

1. Numb the pain

Some people try to avoid grief by numbing its pain. They may use things such as alcohol, narcotics, food, exercise, shopping, or anger.

2. Replace what's lost

There are individuals who try to avoid grief by replacing what was lost. If a woman has lost her marriage, whether it is her choice or her husband's, she may quickly jump into another relationship to replace the emptiness in her life rather than dealing with the pain. If she is experiencing the loss of companionship, she may begin spending an unhealthy amount of time with one of her children, expecting that child to fill that gap. If she's feeling a loss of self-esteem, she might become obsessed with working out, dieting, or cosmetic procedures in an attempt to regain it.

3. Avoid reminders

In an attempt to avoid dealing with the grief caused by betrayal, the wounded spouse may avoid people, places, activities, mementos, or topics that remind her of the pain. While it can be healthy to initially avoid such triggers until some healing has taken place, to continue to do so indefinitely, refusing to address the pain, is not.

4. Staying busy

Packing the schedule by helping others, taking trips, working overtime, or participating in hobbies is another way some attempt to avoid grieving. Perpetually doing anything to occupy the mind or body to avoid facing the pain is unhealthy.

Grief is patient yet persistent. It will not go away simply because it is ignored. Inevitably, it must be faced and processed. There is healing on the other side of the mountain of grief but there is no way to go around it. The only path of healing goes through grief.

Day Two Assignments

In Psalm 55, David grieves because he is surrounded by enemies and one of his closest friends has betrayed him. He tells how this loved one's words were smooth but his heart was so wicked that he betrayed his covenant. David proclaimed that he could have handled being betrayed by an enemy or by someone who hated him. But this betrayal at the hands of someone with whom he had such sweet memories had him in anguish. He poured his heart out to God, and in his anger expressed that he wanted the betrayer destroyed. He also speaks of the pain being so great that he wanted to escape it. Ultimately, he puts his trust in God.

I see so many parallels between David's experience with betrayal and what we who have been betrayed by the sexual acting out of our spouses go through.

Read Psalm 55 and take note of where you can identify with David's pain.

1 Listen to my prayer, O God, do not ignore my plea;
2 hear me and answer me. My thoughts trouble me and I am distraught
3 because of what my enemy is saying, because of the threats of the wicked; for they bring down suffering on me and assail me in their anger.
4 My heart is in anguish within me; the terrors of death have fallen on me.
5 Fear and trembling have beset me; horror has overwhelmed me.
6 I said, "Oh, that I had the wings of a dove! I would fly away and be at rest.
7 I would flee far away and stay in the desert;
8 I would hurry to my place of shelter, far from the tempest and storm."
9 Lord, confuse the wicked, confound their words, for I see violence and strife in the city.
10 Day and night they prowl about on its walls; malice and abuse are within it.
11 Destructive forces are at work in the city; threats and lies never leave its streets.

12 If an enemy were insulting me, I could endure it; if a foe were rising against me, I could hide.

13 But it is you, a man like myself, my companion, my close friend,

14 with whom I once enjoyed sweet fellowship at the house of God, as we walked about among the worshipers.

15 Let death take my enemies by surprise; let them go down alive to the realm of the dead, for evil finds lodging among them.

16 As for me, I call to God, and the LORD saves me.

17 Evening, morning and noon I cry out in distress, and he hears my voice.

18 He rescues me unharmed from the battle waged against me, even though many oppose me.

19 God, who is enthroned from of old, who does not change— he will hear them and humble them, because they have no fear of God.

20 My companion attacks his friends; he violates his covenant.

21 His talk is smooth as butter, yet war is in his heart; his words are more soothing than oil, yet they are drawn swords.

22 Cast your cares on the LORD and he will sustain you; he will never let the righteous be shaken.

23 But you, God, will bring down the wicked into the pit of decay; the bloodthirsty and deceitful will not live out half their days. But as for me, I trust in you.

In today's lesson, we looked at why and how we avoid grief. In Psalm 55, David also wished to flee the pain. In verse six, he tells of his desire to have the wings of a dove so he could escape and fly away.

Have you had thoughts like these? How have you attempted to avoid the grief you've felt because of your husband's sexual sin? _____

_____

_____

_____

_____

_____

_____

_____

Next Step: In Psalm 55, David expressed anger, anguish, a desire to flee, and a desire to see his betrayer punished. But ultimately, David placed his trust in God. If you want to face your pain and experience peace, place your trust in God to see that accomplished. Tell him of your commitment.

Day Three
Unresolved Grief

Grief does not lay dormant or disappear if ignored. Like untreated termites in a home, it eats away at your insides, causing all kinds of destruction. According to counselor and author Robert Taibbe, these are a few possible results of unprocessed grief.

1. Irritability and anger

This may be directed at the offending party or it may spill over onto others. Kristina McMorris, in *Bridge of Scarlett Leaves* writes, "The whole world can become an enemy when you lose what you love."

2. Continued obsession

When the grief caused by sexual betrayal is left unattended, this can lead the wounded spouse to replay the details, the whys and the what-ifs over and over in her mind to the point of obsession.

3. Hyperalertness and fear of loss

The world and everyone in it can feel unsafe to someone who has been betrayed. The anxiety caused by this can lead someone to become paranoid and go to extremes to avoid being hurt again if this pain is not addressed.

4. Behavioral overreaction

The betrayed spouse may overreact to minor stimuli, become overly clingy to the offending spouse or another loved one, or avoid emotional closeness to the spouse or others at all cost. These are examples of some of the behavioral overreactions that might result from unresolved grief.

5. Addictive and self-harming behaviors

Unprocessed grief can become so overwhelming that the individual may become addicted to substances or behaviors used to escape the pain. In the worst case, the individual may inflict harm upon herself with temporary or even permanent results.

6. Apathy, numbness and depression

The emotional psyche can become so overwhelmed with unresolved pain that the individual begins to shut down feelings resulting in a lack of desire to participate or even care about what is going on around her. There can be a "Why bother?" attitude and a desire to be left alone. Left unattended, it can lead to severe depression.

Day Three Assignments

The pain caused by the sexual acting out of a partner can be intense and overwhelming. As tempting as it may be to escape, suppress, or ignore those feelings, unresolved grief can be damaging and can lead to other issues.

1. Have you experienced ongoing anger and irritability? Yes □ No □ If so, is it primarily directed at your spouse or has it been directed at others? _____

2. Have you battled intrusive thoughts or obsessed over the details of your husband's acting out? Yes □ No □

3. Have you become hypervigilant about your husband's behavior, attitude, and activities out of a fear that he will hurt you again? Yes □ No □

4. Have you found yourself overreacting to things your spouse or others have said or done? Yes □ No □

5. Are you concerned that you are in danger of becoming addicted to a substance or behavior you have turned to in your pain? Yes □ No □

6. Have you harmed yourself in any way since discovering your husband's sexual activities? Yes □ No □

7. Do you feel like life has lost its meaning? Yes □ No □

8. Do you feel hopeless? Yes □ No □

9. Have you had thoughts of suicide? Yes □ No □

If you are feeling stuck in your grief or feel so overwhelmed by it that you struggle to function on a daily basis, or if you are having thoughts of suicide, please seek professional help. You have experienced trauma, and there is no shame in admitting you need help moving forward. As difficult as it may be to believe this now, the pain doesn't last forever. You can rediscover true feelings of joy. You can dream new dreams and discover a fresh vision for a great future.

Next Step: Don't put off the grieving process. If you feel stuck in the process or you feel unending despair and depression, ask God to give you comfort and reach out to a professional counselor for help.

Day Four
What to Grieve

The porn or sex addiction of a spouse does not result in just one loss for the wounded partner. Regardless of whether the addict stays or goes, lives in denial or fully embraces recovery, the betrayed wife faces numerous losses. Each loss needs to be acknowledged and grieved. Here are just some of the losses a betrayed spouse my face.

1. Who she thought her husband was

A double life, lies, and deceit are a part of the addicted life. There is a whole other side to the addicted husband that his wife has known nothing about. The person she thought she married is not the person she now knows. That image of her man is gone.

2. What she thought her marriage was

Everything she experienced day to day painted one picture of her marriage. She may have thought she had a great marriage and that they were emotionally connected. Now the reality is that her husband has bonded with other individuals or images. The marriage she thought she had doesn't exist.

3. Life as before

No matter how much healing takes place in the life of the addicted husband, his spouse, and the marriage, life will never be the same as it was before this crisis hit. Life as the wife knew it before is lost.

4. The dream for her future

Almost every woman, when she marries, has a dream for the future of marriage and her family. Rare would be the woman who enters marriage with a dream that includes broken trust, sexual addiction, and ongoing 12-step meetings. The dream she had for her future is gone.

These are just a few of the common losses a wife may experience as a result of discovering her husband's addiction. Others may include loss of emotional security, loss of trust, loss of financial security if the addiction has resulted in loss of job, loss of community standing if the addiction has become public, and the loss of the support of family or friends if the addiction has involved others in that category.

For the wounded spouse to completely heal, she needs to face each of these losses and work through them.

Day Four Assignments

Set aside some time to really think about what you have lost as a result of your husband's sexual acting out. Make a list of those losses.

What I've lost due to my husband's addiction:

1. _____

2. _____

3. _____

4. _____

5. _____

6. _____

7. _____

8. _____

9. _____

Next Step: Surrender these losses to God and trust him to supply your needs physically, emotionally, mentally, and spiritually.

Day Five
Grieving Guideposts

As we saw on Day 1, there is not just one correct way to grieve. Everybody grieves a little differently. What is most important is not *how* you grieve but *that* you grieve. Sigmund Freud spoke of "the work of grief." Grieving is hard and draining work. Though not pleasant at the time, it is a necessary work that serves as a healing balm.

The following are elements of the grieving process that many have found effective.

1. Acknowledge the pain.

In *Macbeth*, Shakespeare wrote, "Give sorrow words; the grief that does not speak knits up the o-er wrought heart and bids it break."

2. Share the pain with someone who's been there.

"Bear one another's burdens, and so fulfill the law of Christ" (Galatians 6:2 ESV). *"Rejoice with those who rejoice, weep with those who weep"* (Romans 12:15 ESV). God never intended for mankind to walk through grief alone. Writer Cheryl Strayed says, "The healing power of even the most microscopic exchange with someone who knows in a flash precisely what you're talking about because she experienced that thing too cannot be overstated."

3. Schedule time to grieve.

Life is busy and doesn't slow down because a crisis entered the picture. The best way to ensure grief doesn't get pushed aside is to schedule time for it. It is best to set a time when others aren't around so it will be time uninterrupted.

4. Set a time limit.

Just as we do not want to ignore grief, neither do we want to be swallowed up by it. As we said, grief is hard work. Limiting the time set aside can help to keep the experience from being completely overwhelming. Obviously, one hour of grieving will not be sufficient to process the pain of betrayal. But limiting the time may make the individual more likely to repeat this process regularly until some real healing can take place.

5. Have a plan.

Knowing how to work through pain is not intuitive. Entering this designated time with a specific plan will best ensure its effectiveness.

6. Ask for God's help.

The Creator of the universe created each of us, so he knows best what we need to heal. Asking for his guidance, comfort, and healing is wise and consoling.

7. Remember the pain won't last forever.

The pain caused by the betrayal of the one person you most love and trust can be so severe and deep that it can be difficult to imagine a time when it won't feel so oppressive. But Psalm 147:3 promises, *"He heals the brokenhearted and binds up their wounds."*

8. Welcome the tears.

There is a therapeutic value to those tears shed in grief. Dr. William H. Frey, a biochemist and tear expert, explains that reflex tears, such as result from an eye irritant, are 98% water, but that emotional tears contain stress hormones and other toxins which accumulate during stress. Shedding those tears not only rids the body of those toxins, it also stimulates the production of endorphins.

9. Focus more on what is left than what is lost.

Life is never all good and it is never all bad. Though much may be lost, there are things left for which to be thankful. And there are certain things in life no one can take away.

10. Make a gratitude list.

As stated under number nine, not everything is lost. Making a list of things for which to be grateful changes not only the focus, it can change the mood. *"In everything give thanks; for this is God's will for you in Christ Jesus"* (1 Thessalonians 5:18 NASB).

Day Five Assignments

This has been a difficult week as we delved into grief. How I wish I could whisk each of you past the pain. But walking through the grieving process is normal, necessary, therapeutic, and blessed. Shakespeare said, "To weep is to make less the depth of grief." Take some time to work through the grief. Try the things below. It won't take away all of your grief but it is a start.

1. Set aside at least one time to grieve this week.

2. Set a timer (30-60 minutes).

3. Ask God to help you process your feelings and to comfort you.

4. Journal about your feelings.

5. Write a good-bye letter to the life you had and the spouse you thought you knew.

6. List three things you have left for which you can give thanks.

7. Thank God for those blessings.

Next Step: Setting aside a time to grieve will not erase all of your pain, but it is a start. Commit to that small start. Do it again the next week. And again after that. Continue until the fog begins to lift and you see the dawn of a brighter day.

WEEK ELEVEN
Freedom through Forgiveness

"To forgive is to set a prisoner free and discover that the prisoner was you.

- Lewis B. Smedes

Day One
Imprisoned

There may be no facet of the betrayal by a sexually addicted husband that is more difficult than forgiveness. The deep wounds inflicted are not merely the consequence of a single offensive act. They are the results of the repeated deception and duplicity of the addict. How can someone forgive such cruelty?

Corrie ten Boom told of the experience she had in 1947 when she spoke on forgiveness in a church in Munich. After the service, a man approached her whom she immediately recognized as a guard in the concentration camp where she and her sister Betsie were confined after being arrested for concealing Jews in their home during the Nazi occupation of Holland.

Her mind was flooded with the memories of the atrocities they and others experienced at the hands of this man. Now he stood before her, telling her what a fine message on forgiveness she had presented. He proceeded to tell her that since that time as a guard, he had become a Christian. He said he knew God had forgiven him for the cruel things he'd done there. Then he said, "I would like to hear it from your lips as well." He stretched out his hand and said, "Will you forgive me?"

Corrie ten Boom recounted, "I stood there – whose sins had every day to be forgiven – and could not. Betsie had died in that place – could he erase her slow terrible death simply for the asking? It could not have been many seconds that he stood there, hand held out, but to me it seemed hours as I wrestled with the most difficult thing I had ever to do.'"

She went on to explain that she knew she had to forgive him because God's condition for forgiving us is that we forgive those who have injured us. *"Jesus said, 'If you do not forgive men their trespasses, neither will your Father forgive your trespasses'"* (Matthew 6:15 NKJV).

Furthermore, she had seen that those who had forgiven their former enemies were able to return to the outside world and rebuild their lives. But those who refused to forgive remained bitter invalids.

"Jesus, help me!" she silently prayed. "I can lift my hand. I can do that much. You supply the feeling."

As she continued the story, she said, "And so woodenly, mechanically, I thrust my hand into the one stretched out to me. And as I did, an incredible thing took place. The current started in my shoulder, raced down my arm, sprang into our joined hands. And then this healing warmth seemed to flood my whole being, bringing tears to my eyes."

Then she said, "I forgive you, brother! With all my heart!"

Corrie ten Boom was no longer a prisoner in a concentration camp. But she realized that if she refused to forgive, she would be imprisoned in bitterness. You have been deeply wounded by the actions of your spouse. Forgiving him may feel like the most difficult thing you've ever faced. The alternative is a life of bitterness and misery. Forgiveness is the key that unlocks the chains shackling your future of peace. This week, we will explore how it is possible to forgive the seemingly unforgivable.

Day One Assignments

You have been incredibly wounded by the sexual betrayal of your spouse. You may never face a more difficult task than forgiving in the midst of such pain. Forgiveness is further complicated by the many misconceptions of what it actually entails. Hopefully through our study this week, we will clear things up enough that you can move forward with forgiveness, if you've been unable to do so to this point. For now, let's consider your current feelings regarding forgiving your spouse.

Check up to three statements that best describe you at this time.

____ I can never imagine forgiving my spouse for the pain he has caused me.

____ I hope I can forgive my spouse at some point, but it will be way out in the future.

____ I may be able to forgive my spouse, but I can't stay in relationship with him.

____ I would like to forgive my spouse but I'm afraid he'll hurt me again.

____ I thought I forgave my spouse but I'm not sure because I still wrestle with anger and pain.

____ I can't forgive my spouse because he has not apologized or shown remorse.

____ I will forgive my spouse when he makes up for what he's done to me.

____ I forgave my spouse quickly because I know that's what God commands me to do.

____ My husband doesn't deserve my forgiveness.

____ I feel like I've truly forgiven my spouse and I feel at peace now.

Next Step: Ask God to give you an honest understanding of where you are in the process of forgiving your spouse. Ask him to give you a willingness to ultimately forgive as he desires you to and ask him to give you the wisdom and grace to get there.

Day Two
It's Not What You Think

There may be a number of reasons why a wounded spouse won't forgive her betrayer. We will consider several later this week. Often, failure to forgive stems from a lack of understanding about what it means to forgive. Today I will attempt to clear up some confusion by explaining 10 things that are not a part of forgiveness.

1. Forgiveness is not always quick.

Unquestionably, God's command is to forgive. But certainly, he understands that there are times when this will be extremely difficult. His command is given for our good because he knows what an unwillingness to forgive does to our bodies, minds, and spirits. Unfortunately, many religious communities do a disservice to some deeply wounded individuals by guilting them into attempting to forgive before they have had time to adequately process their pain.

2. Forgiveness is not condoning the offense.

In forgiving a spouse for sexual betrayal, you are not condoning or downplaying the severity of what has been done to you. Those actions are sinful, and they are grievous to you and to God. They must not be minimized.

3. Forgiveness is not allowing others to take advantage of you.

It is possible to completely forgive someone while still putting boundaries in place to protect yourself and lessen the likelihood of a recurrence.

4. Forgiveness is not a feeling.

Forgiveness is an act of the will and is not conditioned upon a feeling. The feeling may come in time. But, I dare say, often those who have been deeply wounded and forgive anyway, don't do it because they *feel* like forgiving.

5. Forgiveness is not the same as trust.

A mother can forgive someone who hurt her child but never trust that person to babysit again. We can forgive our spouses for betraying us sexually, but the trust may not be restored for a while. Pastor and writer Dave Willis says, "You don't have to trust someone in order to forgive them, but you do have to forgive in order to make trust possible again."

6. Forgiveness is not a pain eraser.

The absence of pain is not necessarily an indication of forgiveness. Because forgiveness is not predicated upon feelings, it is possible to forgive while still wrestling with lingering pain. When a doctor removes a cancerous tumor, the healing begins immediately, though the pain remains. Similarly, forgiveness removes the "tumor," but the wound must be allowed the necessary time to heal.

7. Forgiveness is not the same as reconciliation.

It is possible to forgive someone without restoring the relationship. Reconciliation is not always possible or even wise. In the case of sexual addiction, the addict may choose the addiction over the relationship by either walking away or by failing to pursue the recovery that is the necessary foundation for restoring the marriage.

8. Forgiveness is not conditioned upon remorse or an apology.

Ultimately, God commands us to forgive...period. Even as Jesus looked upon those who were crucifying him, he prayed, *"Father, forgive them, for they do not know what they are doing"* (Luke 23:34). Jesus forgave them despite their lack of remorse. On Day One, we read that verse that tells us that if we don't forgive others, God won't forgive us. His command is not dismissive of our pain. To the contrary, God knows that our refusal to forgive sentences us to a life of pain. Withholding forgiveness until we receive an apology or see remorse is to relinquish control of our peace and future to another.

9. Forgiveness is not cheap.

The cost of your husband's betrayal is so great, there is no way he can make up for the pain he has caused. It cost Jesus his life to cover our betrayal. None of us can pay him back for that.

10. Forgiveness is not forgetting.

God promises, *"I will forgive their wickedness and will remember their sins no more"* (Hebrews 8:12). It is not that God has chosen amnesia, but forgiveness at the deepest level. He has cancelled our debt by meeting our sin with mercy. He commands us to forgive in the same way. Forgiveness is spiritual. Forgetting is biological. God has not given us the ability to literally forget an offense. The point of forgiveness is not to forget the offense, but to remember it with God's grace.

Day Two Assignments

Forgiveness is such a beautiful concept. We certainly welcome it when we have made a mistake, acted inappropriately, or hurt someone else. But forgiveness becomes difficult when we are the ones that have been severely wounded. C.S. Lewis said it like this: "Everyone thinks forgiveness is a lovely idea until he has something to forgive." Forgiveness can seem even more difficult when we believe it to be something it is not.

Forgiveness is not quick. It is not condoning the offense. It is not allowing others to take advantage of us. It is not a feeling. It is not the same as trusting. It is not a pain eraser. It is not the same as reconciliation. It is not conditioned upon an apology or remorse. It is not cheap. And it is not forgetting.

The enemy knows that if we refuse to forgive, we will become bitter and will be unable to fulfill the destiny God has for us. What better way to hurt the Father than to cripple his children? We are more likely to remain unforgiving if we believe these falsehoods.

Have you found it difficult to forgive because of any of the misconceptions about forgiveness we looked at today? Yes □ No □

Explain how one of these misconceptions has been a stumbling block in your life to forgiveness. _____
_____
_____
_____
_____
_____

Now recognizing that this misconception is not a component of forgiveness, does forgiveness seem a little more possible? Yes □ No □

Next Step: What obstacle stands between you and your willingness to forgive your spouse? Surrender that to God.

Day Three
Forgiveness Clarified

You have been on a recovery journey for at least the past 10 weeks if you have been working through this material. Sexual betrayal has wounded you, but you don't have to live in that pain. You can heal and embrace a healthier future regardless of the path your spouse has chosen. But unforgiveness will be a roadblock to a brighter future. Nelson Mandela was right: "When a deep injury is done us, we never recover until we forgive."

On Day Two, we looked at what forgiveness is not. Now let's look at what forgiveness is.

1. Forgiveness is a command.

"Bear with each other and forgive one another if any of you has a grievance against someone. Forgive as the Lord forgave you" (Colossians 3:13).

2. Forgiveness is a choice.

We saw yesterday that forgiveness is not a feeling. We don't wait until we no longer feel angry or hurt to forgive. We don't wait until we feel like forgiving. We can choose to forgive regardless of how we feel. Corrie ten Boom said, "Forgiveness is an act of the will, and the will can function regardless of the temperature of the heart."

3. Forgiveness is possible.

In the depths of betrayal trauma, it might be impossible to imagine ever being able to forgive your spouse. But God would not command us to do something that is impossible to do. It will likely be impossible to do it in our own strength. God promises to give us the strength we need. *"I can do all things through Christ who strengthens me"* (Philippians 4:13 KJV).

4. Forgiveness is healing.

Unforgiveness is classified in medical books as a disease. According to Dr. Steven Standiford, chief of surgery at the Cancer Treatment Centers of America, refusing to forgive makes people sick and keeps them that way. Because God commands forgiveness, to remain in unforgiveness is sin. There are times when this can make us physically sick. King David said, *"Because of your anger, my whole body is sick; my health is broken because of my sins"* (Psalm 38:3 NLT).

5. Forgiveness is canceling a debt.

There is not anything a betraying spouse can do to make up for the pain he has caused – even with the highest intention and effort. Forgiveness is cancelling that debt – sending it away.

6. Forgiveness is an act of trusting God.

We have no right or authority to judge another or to exact justice. God promises that he is just and will deal appropriately with each person based on the choices they make. *"Don't insist on getting even; that's not for you to do. 'I'll do the judging.' says God. 'I'll take care of it'"* (Romans 12:19 MSG). When we forgive, we are releasing that person into God's hands and trusting him to deal with the offending person as he deems best.

7. Forgiveness is both an event and a process.

I love the words of Paula Rinehart, author of *Strong Women, Soft Hearts*. "Forgiveness is both an event and a process – a big 'Yes, I choose to forgive,' followed by many little yeses as the months and years roll by."

Day Three Assignments

How does it make you feel to hear that forgiveness is a choice, an act of the will? _____
_____
_____

Has there been a time during this betrayal trauma that it has felt like it would be impossible to forgive your spouse? Yes □ No □

Do you believe God can give you the strength to forgive your spouse? Yes □ No □

Can you see how forgiveness could result in you feeling better physically? Yes □ No □

Do you trust that God knows how to best deal with your spouse for the things he has done that have hurt you and your family? Yes □ No □

What do you think of Paula Rinehart's description about forgiveness being both an event and a process? _____
_____
_____
_____

Next Step: If you are struggling with forgiving your spouse, ask God to help you to trust him to deal with your husband in the best way. Surrender your spouse to God.

Day Four
Why Not Forgive?

A little boy was sitting on a park bench in obvious pain. A man walking by asked him what was wrong. The young boy said, "I'm sitting on a bumble bee." The man urgently asked, "Then why don't you get up?" The boy replied, "Because I figure I'm hurting him more than he is hurting me."

There may be a number of reasons why we may choose not to forgive our spouses for the pain they've caused us. But if we could sum it up in one sentence, I think our reasoning would sound similar to that of the little boy: We think we are hurting our spouses more by remaining in our unforgiveness than if we were to move from that position. In reality, we keep ourselves in pain.

The following are just a few of the possible reasons a wounded spouse may refuse to forgive her husband:

1. She is afraid he will forget what he's done.

To remain angry or wounded keeps the matter before her husband and serves as an ever present reminder as to what he has done. Unfortunately, it also keeps it in the forefront of her mind, preventing her from moving forward in healing.

2. She wants to see him pay for what he has done.

If she can make him miserable by not forgiving him, at least she knows he is experiencing some repercussion for what he's done. If she releases him to God, she may not be able to visibly see him suffering for hurting her.

3. She wants him to be accountable so he won't hurt her again.

By not forgiving, she may feel in control of her spouse's recovery and choices. She may only dole out measures of forgiveness or approval as he performs as she requires. She is operating under the false assumption that she really can control his actions, therefore thinking she can prevent him from acting out and hurting her again.

4. She thinks forgiving makes her vulnerable.

Forgiveness is not a sign of weakness. To the contrary, it takes great strength to forgive such grievous betrayal. Mahatma Gandhi said, "The weak never forgive. Forgiveness is the attribute of the strong."

5. She is afraid she'll lose leverage.

If she can convince her spouse that he has to earn her forgiveness, she feels she has the power in the relationship, keeping her from feeling out of control.

6. She feels justified in her unforgiveness.

Certainly, sexual betrayal causes deep trauma and to the human eye does not compare to something such as an unkind word spoken. In man's rating system, unfaithfulness ranks much higher than most other offenses. However, when we compare ourselves to a perfect God, we all fall miserably short. When we remember all the forgiveness we've received from a holy God, we as imperfect people have no basis for failing to extend the grace we've been given.

7. She doesn't recognize that it is poisoning her own soul.

It has been said that "holding onto resentment is like drinking poison and waiting for the other person to die."

Day Four Assignments

It is easy when you've been wounded so deeply, to only remember the things your spouse has done to hurt you. It is important to also remember the things he has done right. Think about anything else that has kept you from forgiving your spouse. Look back over those things listed in the lesson today.

Are you afraid that if you forgive your spouse, he will forget what he's done and how much it hurt you? Yes □ No □

Do you want to continue to hold out on forgiving so you can make your spouse pay for what he's done to you? Yes □ No □

Are you trying to make your spouse earn your forgiveness as a way to control his sobriety, hoping it will prevent him from acting out again and hurting you? Yes □ No □

Do you feel like you will appear weak to your spouse if you forgive him? Yes □ No □

Do you feel like others may think you are weak if you forgive your spouse? Yes □ No □

Do you think you will lose leverage in your relationship if you forgive your spouse? Yes □ No □

Do you think your spouse has hurt you so severely that he doesn't deserve your forgiveness? Yes □ No □

Do you think holding on to resentment is hurting your spouse more than it is hurting you? Yes □ No □

Next Step: Holding on to unforgiveness will eventually destroy you. Turn your palms toward heaven and release those barriers standing in your way to God.

Day Five
How to Forgive

We have spent this week attempting to better understand forgiveness and the roadblocks that may stand in its way. But even the greatest understanding of the issue will not make forgiving sexual betrayal easy. Today we will consider a number of suggestions that may help in this process.

1. Pray for God's help.

There is no doubt that forgiving your spouse for how he's betrayed you may be one of the toughest things you've ever had to do. As we saw on Day Three, God stands ready to provide you with the strength to do so. Simply ask him.

2. Remember your own faults.

We are all flawed individuals with many character defects. Your faults in no way justify his actions. But the Bible says that we should treat others the way we would like to be treated (Matthew 7:12).

3. Separate the offense from the offender.

The mistakes of your spouse, even as bad as they may be, do not define who he is as a person. He is a precious child of God who made bad choices. That does not make him a bad person.

4. Remember what forgiveness is.

Forgiveness is a choice, not a feeling. It is trusting God to deal with your spouse in the best way. And it is your ticket to freedom and healing.

5. Don't nurse your wounds.

Continuing to ruminate on what your spouse has done to you is like constantly picking at a scab. The wound won't heal and you risk infection.

A Lutheran pastor, when talking to Corrie ten Boom about forgiveness, likened it to ringing a big church bell with a rope. "When we forgive someone, we take our hand off the rope. But if we've been tugging at our grievances for a long time, we mustn't be surprised if the old angry thoughts keep coming for a while. They're just the ding-dongs of the old bell slowing down."

6. Recognize the personal benefits.

Remember that forgiveness is a gift you give to yourself. When you forgive your spouse, you open the door for your own mental, physical, and spiritual health and well-being. It is the ultimate example of self-care.

7. Pray blessings on the one who has hurt you.

Don't wait for the feelings of forgiveness to come before praying for your spouse to be blessed. Feelings are like the caboose of a train. They don't drive the train. Forgiveness is the motor that drives the train. Make the choice to forgive, begin praying blessings over your spouse, and watch the feelings in your heart eventually line up with that action.

Day Five Assignments

To live in unforgiveness is to allow what has happened to you in the past to control you in your future. T.D. Jakes says, "Forgiveness is about empowering yourself, rather than empowering your past." Begin empowering yourself today through the power of forgiveness.

1. Make a list of the ways in which your spouse has hurt you. _____
_____
_____
_____
_____
_____
_____
_____
_____
_____
_____
_____
_____

2. Ask God to help you forgive your spouse.

3. Thank God for all the times he has forgiven you.

4. Sit in a chair with an empty chair in front of you. Picture your spouse in that chair.

5. Referring to your list of the ways in which your spouse has hurt you (#1 above), with each offense say, "I forgive you for _____
_____
_____ and I love you."

6. Make a list of things about your spouse for which you are grateful. ___
_____
_____
_____

_____

_____

_____

7. Ask God to bless your spouse.

Next Step: As we saw on Day Three, forgiveness is both an event and a process. Today's assignment is the start. Continue to choose forgiveness daily. Ask God for the wisdom to know when you should communicate that forgiveness to your spouse.

WEEK TWELVE
Letting Go and Moving On

"Holding on is believing that there's only a past;
letting go is knowing that there's a future."

- Daphne Rose Kingma

Day One
Let Go or Get Dragged

It was a beautiful, sunny day and I was excited for a new adventure. I was going water skiing with my best friend and her family. After enjoying my time in the boat watching others, it was my turn. It looked fun and didn't appear to be too difficult. I was given last minute instructions including the reminder to let go of the rope if I fell. Got it! Ready to go.

I began by sitting in the water and holding the rope as the boat slowly increased its speed. I got up! Briefly. But then I fell. I knew I had been told to let go of the rope but in that moment, I panicked. I would be left alone in the water if I let go. That rope seemed like my lifeline, so I hung on with all my strength. That would prove to be a bad decision.

What ensued was what I imagine it feels like to be placed on a torture rack and have my arms stretched, while simultaneously being slapped in the face and water boarded. I must have significantly reduced the water level in the lake by the amount of water I snorted that day. I eventually did let go after everyone in the boat was screaming, "Let go of the rope!"

That was my one and only time to ever attempt water skiing.

You likely started your marriage with great excitement as you anticipated the adventure before you. You probably never imagined that the one who stood before you and pledged his eternal love for you could wound you so deeply. How can you ever get over sexual betrayal? I don't think you ever really get over it but you can get through it and even come out stronger than before. How is that possible?

At some point, you have to make the decision to let go of the past or let it drag you through the rest of your life as ongoing torture. It is important that you come to that decision on your own. Don't attempt to move on due to pressure from your spouse or anyone else. And while letting go and moving on is critical, you need to make sure you have adequately processed the pain from betrayal.

This week we will look at some of the things necessary to move on in a healthy way.

Day One Assignments

Roy T. Bennett, author of *The Light in the Heart*, said, "Once you realize you deserve a bright future, letting go of your dark past is the best choice you will ever make." Jeremiah 29:11 says, *"'For I know the plans I have for you,' declares the Lord, 'Plans to prosper you and not to harm you, plans to give you a hope and a future.'"* God has a good plan for your life that was not nullified by the bad things that have transpired.

1. Does letting go of the dark past of betrayal seem doable? Does it seem scary? Explain. _____

_____

_____

_____

_____

_____

2. Have you come to the place that you can believe you deserve a brighter future? That it is possible? Explain. _____

_____

_____

_____

_____

Next Step: Letting go is a choice. That choice is made easier when we believe God has a good plan for our lives. If you are struggling with believing that, ask God to help you and then make that choice by faith.

Day Two
Set Yourself Free

One of the Webster definitions of release is the act of setting free or letting go. When you let go of the past, you free yourself to move on and take hold of a better future. C.S. Lewis said it this way: "Getting over a painful experience is much like crossing monkey bars. You have to let go at some point in order to move forward."

Here are some things to let go of:

1. Hurts

Don't be a hoarder of hurts. A hoarder is someone who has difficulty discarding things regardless of their value or the negative impact it may have on his or her life. The person usually experiences great anxiety at the thought of letting an item go, often fearing he may need it in the future. Holding a hurt can initially serve you. Aside from being a legitimate response to betrayal, the hurt can be a useful defense mechanism or powerful tool for leverage. But when it remains, it works like Velcro to which future hurts stick and accumulate. Let us behave like Teflon that can take the heat without allowing the hurt to stick to us.

2. Life as it Was

Getting stuck in the past, whether that past was good or bad, keeps you from enjoying the present or the future. In order to have a better future you have to quit trying to have a better past. Often, the good old days weren't really as good as we remember anyway. In the presence of sexual addiction, while not everything was an illusion, the family unit was certainly not as healthy as it can be after recovery.

3. Yesterday's Dreams

American Professor of Literature Joseph Campbell said, "We must be willing to let go of the life we've planned, so as to have the life that is waiting for us." Hopefully you've taken time to grieve the loss of those dreams. Now it is time to let go of those dreams that are no longer possible so you can embrace what's next.

4. Mistakes and Failures

As a betrayed spouse, it is natural to be haunted by your own mistakes or failures surrounding the betrayal, possibly wrestling with questions like, "Why wasn't I stronger?" or "Why did I behave that way?" A better question would be, "How have I grown though this experience?" or "What have I learned about myself?" Writer and blogger Melanie Koulouris said, "There is no sense in punishing your future for the mistakes of your past. Forgive yourself, grow from it, and then let it go."

Day Two Assignments

Author Havelock Ellis said, "All the art of living lies in a fine mingling of letting go and holding on." After the discovery of betrayal, it can be easy to fall into an all or nothing mentality, believing that if all was not what you had believed it to be then nothing was as you believed it to be. But the reality is that there were likely many good things in your life, marriage, and family that are worth holding on to. Hold on to God. Hold on to the good memories. Hold on to hope. At the same time, life exactly as you knew it is gone, some dreams are lost forever, and disappointments and pain now remain. Let go of the pain. Let go of the life you once knew. Let go of past dreams that are no longer viable. Let go of past mistakes and failures.

1. List two results of betrayal that you have yet to sufficiently grieve.

_____

_____

2. List two results of betrayal that you have grieved but aren't sure you are ready to release.

_____

_____

3. List two results of betrayal that you have grieved and you are ready to release.

_____

_____

Next Step: Mr. Ellis was right. The art of living is knowing what to let go of and what to hold on to. Ask God for the wisdom to know the difference and the strength to accomplish it.

Day Three
A Piece to Peace

Letting go of the past does not erase it from your memory. But it does affect your focus. I like the analogy of a vehicle to focus. A car has a large windshield but a small rearview mirror. Our gaze is forward. Our glance is backward. The Bible says it like this: *"Let your eyes look straight ahead; fix your gaze directly before you."* (Proverbs 4:25).

Our past should serve as a teacher, not a torturer. Author Shannon L. Alder said, "Forget what hurt you but never forget what it taught you."

On our final three days, we will look at tips for letting go and moving on.

1. Choose to forgive.

We spent a week looking at the subject of forgiveness. It would be nice if that were sufficient time to master it. That process takes time. But to remain in unforgiveness is like trying to move forward with heavy weights on. It's possible but not easy.

2. Be more realistic.

Happily ever after exists only in fairy tales. It's not real life. Between fairy tales and Facebook, it is easy to have an unrealistic picture of life and marriage. The only couple that has a perfect marriage is the couple you don't know well enough. There are no perfect marriages because there are no perfect people. Recognizing that hurts, even deep wounds, are a part of life can make it easier to let them go when they do happen.

3. Accept what is.

The final stage of grieving is acceptance. Your life may not be what you hoped for or what you thought it was, but it is what it is. Coming to terms with that is a key to letting go of what it is not and moving on.

Day Three Assignments

We have a dear friend who used to drive a race car. It can be scary to ride with him now because he drives confidently and aggressively. He does that because he knows cars and how to drive in a way that most do not.

A race car offers a good analogy on focus. If it goes into a skid, the driver knows to focus on where he wants the car to go and not on the wall he wants to avoid. In fear, an inexperienced driver will focus on the object he wants to avoid. A professional knows that we tend to steer in the direction of our focus, even if we don't want to.

Do you want to move on in your life? Stop focusing on the past. Choose to forgive. Be more realistic in your expectations about life and marriage. Accept your life as it is instead of lamenting what it is not.

1. Is unforgiveness keeping you from letting go and moving on? Explain where you are in the process of forgiving. _____
_____
_____
_____
_____

2. Do you feel like your expectations for your life are realistic or do you tend to look at others' lives and wish your life was more like theirs? Explain. _____
_____
_____
_____

3. Have you worked through the stages of grief and arrived in a place of acceptance? Yes ☐ No ☐ If not, where are you in that process? _____
_____
_____
_____
_____
_____

Next Step: Your life will follow your focus. Are you focusing on the past or on the future? Ask God to direct your focus in accordance with his will.

Day Four
Take the Challenge

In yesterday's lesson, we began looking at tips for letting go of the past so you can move on with your life. We considered the power of forgiveness, the need to be more realistic, and the benefit of accepting things as they are currently. Today we will focus on three more ideas for letting go and moving on.

1. Challenge unproductive thinking.

Dwelling on the past is like picking at a scab and expecting it to heal. Philippians 4:8 says, *"Finally, brothers and sisters, whatever is true, whatever is noble, whatever is right, whatever is pure, whatever is lovely, whatever is admirable – if anything is excellent or praiseworthy – think about such things."* While it may be true that your spouse sexually betrayed you, is that a thought that meets the other criteria of this verse? Did his unfaithfulness cause colossal consequences? Likely it did. Does dwelling on the fall-out enhance your future? Certainly not.

While there is definitely a time for acknowledging, processing, and grieving these things, there comes a time when you must let these things go if you want to move on. Continuing to dwell in the past will keep you anchored there. God has a good, pleasing and perfect plan for your future. Unproductive thinking is not the road that will lead you there. Recalculate your GPS, renew your mind, and you'll be heading in the right direction for better tomorrows.

2. Discard evidence of past betrayal.

Many women experience years of feeling crazy because they are married to sex addicts who deny it. It is not uncommon for these women to spend countless hours searching for proof to verify their suspicions. When evidence finally comes to light, it can be tempting to hang on to it. After all, this confirms their intuition and validates their sanity.

I suggest any evidence eventually be destroyed. Looking at things such as letters, text messages, pictures, browser histories, or anything that verifies a husband's acting out, can be triggering and destructive. If there is a legal or financial reason she may need these to protect her future, I suggest the information be stored in a safety deposit box, in the attic, or given to a trusted friend. Hanging on to these items can keep the wounded spouse stuck in the past.

3. Change the narrative of your story.

You can choose to look at the horrific things your spouse has done to you and play the victim in the story. Or, you can look at those same things and choose to be the victor in the story. You can adopt the narrative that says, "I am a victim of rejection and betrayal." Or you can change that narrative to, "My husband had a sickness that led him to make poor choices but I am using this as an opportunity to become a stronger, healthier person." It's your story.

Day Four Assignments

Author and speaker Steve Maraboli said, "Incredible change happens in your life when you decide to take control of what you do have power over instead of craving control over what you don't." You don't have control over your past or your spouse but you do have control over how you think about these. You have the power to challenge unproductive thinking and to get rid of reminders of hurtful experiences.

1. On a scale of one to ten, with one being very little negative and unproductive thinking and ten being very excessive, unproductive thinking, where were you when you began this recovery journey?

    1   2   3   4   5   6   7   8   9   10

Where are you now?

    1   2   3   4   5   6   7   8   9   10

2. Do you have a plan in place to counter negative and unproductive thinking? If so, what is it? _____
_____
_____
_____

3. Gather any physical evidence that you have of your husband's acting out. Pray for God's strength to destroy it. If you can't bring yourself to do that yet or if there is some legal reason you may need it in the future, put it away in a safety deposit box, attic, or some other place where you can't easily look at it.

4. Write a one sentence summary of your story in which you are victorious. _____
_____
_____
_____

Next Step: Remember, you can't let go and move on if you are tethered to the past. Ask God to free you, refrain from doing those things which set you back, and keep moving forward toward wholeness.

Day Five
A New Thing

"Forget the former things; do not dwell on the past. See, I am doing a new thing! Now it springs up; do you not perceive it? I am making a way in the wilderness and streams in the wasteland" (Isaiah 43:18-19). This passage captures the essence of this week's theme. We've spent the last few days looking at tips for letting go of the past. What's next?

Aristotle once postulated "horror vacui," meaning nature abhors a vacuum – an empty space. When your life has been ravaged by sexual betrayal and you've worked diligently toward healing so you can let it go and move on, God's plan is not to leave you bare and empty. He's doing a new thing now. To move on from the past ...

1. Enjoy the present.

While it is true that life as you knew it before the discovery of sexual betrayal is over, your life is not over. Focusing on the past can be agonizing. Worrying about the future can cause anxiety. Concentrate on today. *"This is the day the Lord has made; we will rejoice and be glad in it"* (Psalm 118:24). Yesterday is gone. There is no promise of tomorrow. There are things in your life today for which to be grateful. Look for them. Enjoy them.

2. Create and embrace the new.

Replace the old with the new. The brain is a curious and fascinating organ that responds positively to new things. When we are exposed to something new, our brains release endorphins that make us feel better. (It is one of the things that drives the porn addict to seek new images. Satan always attempts to hijack and use for destruction what God intends for good.) Create new experiences to replace the memories of those lost.

a. Learn a new craft or skill. This can be a good form of self-care in addition to creating new memories.

b. Visit new places. Try new restaurants or a new vacation spot.

c. Make new traditions. Past holiday traditions may now be tainted. Brainstorm for new ones.

d. Dream new dreams. Ask God to give you a new vision and dream for your life to replace those lost.

Day Five Assignments

This week we looked at tips for letting go of the past. Today we looked at the need to enjoy the present as you create new memories.

1. God made this day and it is full of beauty and wonder. Name one thing from today for which to give thanks. _____

_____

2. What new hobby, skill, or craft would you like to learn? _____

_____

3. Make a plan to pursue that hobby, skill, or craft.

4. Name a new place you'd like to visit. _____

_____

5. Imagine your life five years from now as a healthy and happy person and write down what that would look like. _____

_____
_____
_____
_____
_____
_____
_____

Next Step: Letting go of the past and moving on includes creating and embracing the new. Ask God to give you a new dream for your life. Make creating new memories a regular part of your life.